50 STATES OF TERROR

The Plot to Cripple America

Marc Neerman

Dedication

This book is dedicated to the men and women who put their lives on the line every day, without recognition or reward, to keep us all safe.

Acknowledgment

iv

To Judy, without whose love and support, this work would have never happened. She completes my world.

CONTENTS

Dedication...iii

Acknowledgment...iv

Chapter One 1

Chapter Two:.. 5

Chapter Three 13

Chapter Four 17

Chapter Five 21

Chapter Six... 27

Chapter Seven 47

Chapter Eight... 58

Chapter Nine 65

Chapter Ten.. 72

Chapter Eleven... 75

Chapter Twelve 82

Chapter Thirteen.. 86

Chapter Fourteen... 91

Chapter Fifteen 100

Chapter Sixteen 107

Chapter Seventeen 126

Chapter Eighteen 133

Chapter Nineteen..141

Chapter Twenty..145

Chapter Twenty-One 149

Chapter Twenty-Two 157

Chapter Twenty-Three..161

Chapter Twenty-Four..170

Chapter Twenty-Five...175

Chapter Twenty-Six...179

Chapter Twenty-Seven 183

Chapter Twenty-Eight 193

Chapter Twenty-Nine 200

Chapter Thirty..205

Chapter Thirty-One...209

Chapter Thirty-Two 213

Chapter Thirty-Three 217

Chapter Thirty-Four..222

Chapter Thirty-Five...230

Chapter Thirty-Six 234

Chapter Thirty-Seven 241

Chapter Thirty-Eight 247

Chapter Thirty-Nine 256

Chapter Forty 261

Chapter Forty-One 270

Chapter Forty-Two 278

Chapter Forty-Three 288

Chapter Forty-Four 298

Chapter Forty-Five 309

About The Author 320

Page Blank Intentionally

Chapter One

He wasn't good-looking. He wasn't particularly tall, maybe 5 feet 8 or nine. He was of medium build and dressed casually. He was in economy class, and the other passengers were not paying any attention to him. After all, what should they? The Aeromexico flight had left Paris at around 11 PM. It was due to arrive at about 4:30 in the morning. Unfortunately, the actual flight was over 12 hours long. He picked a nonstop flight as he did not wish to get his luggage misplaced. He slept as well as he could, as he wished to arrive fresh. It was going to be a long day, and his work was very important.

This trip was the culmination of months of planning and considerable resources. He would have his revenge. As the huge plane arrived at Benito Juarez International Airport in Mexico City, the man smiled and looked forward to the completion of his mission, the destruction of the United States. While he knew he could not actually destroy the country, this mission would destroy America's pride and sense of security. It would cause every American to feel unsafe and insecure. The American people would no longer trust their government to protect them.

The big aircraft taxied to Terminal Two and found the open gate. Two men in reflective vests use their orange cone flashlights to direct the aircraft into the gate. Within a minute or two of the plane being stopped, the fasten seatbelt sign went off. The man took his time getting out of his seat; he did not wish to draw any attention to himself.

He was just an average man on an average flight. He took his one bag out from the overhead compartment and waited in line to exit the aircraft. Exiting with a smile on his face. He knew this was the beginning of the final phase of his project. He also knew that he could never kill as many Americans as he wanted to. However, even though the body count of his project would be less than the number of deaths that occurred on 9/11, he knew this mission would accomplish more.

He walked through the terminal looking at different stores. He had no time for souvenirs, nor did he wish to leave any type of paper trail. Even his airline ticket was purchased with cash. He did stop to get a cup of hot coffee. The coffee was strong and helped the man to wake up. He continued walking, following the signs to the car rental counters. He walked up to the Firefly rental booth. There, he rented a Dodge Grand Caravan. This vehicle will provide him with ample space for people and equipment, if that becomes necessary. It would also blend in busy traffic in the area. This was a mere $80 a day. While he would have it for several weeks, he was not worried about the expense. He had more than enough money to cover the rental, but since he used a fake passport, credit card, and driver's license, he doubted he would ever have to pay for the rental.

He exited the airport and proceeded to the car rental lot. He easily found the vehicle he had just rented. He walked around the vehicle, noticing any type of distinctive damage, which would make his vehicle easier to spot. The vehicle was in good condition and clean. He allowed himself a small smile as he got into the vehicle. He drove the vehicle out of the lot and proceeded north on Avenue 613. Proceeded to Central Avenue. He turned right on Avenue 608 and proceeded to Central Avenue. He drove north for several miles, enjoying looking at the people in the shops. They had no idea who he was, what he was about to do. When he reached Route 57D, he proceeded northwest. This would be a long drive, but he did not wish to check into a hotel along the route and have to display his identification. If he gets tired, you always pull over and take a nap in the back of the van. He continued on through San Cristobal and was amazed at the density of traffic in the area. He would not have to worry about being seen among thousands of cars on the highway. He drove on and decided to get something to eat. The town of El Llano was only a few minutes away, and he decided he should have lunch. He stopped at Enchiladas Nena. His Mexican contact told him it was a good place for lunch and out-of-the-way from prying eyes. The food was excellent, and after lunch, he proceeded on his trip. He continued north through Colonia Julian Villagran and Colonia Benito Juarez. Like many other countries, the name of this famous leader was found throughout the country. As the 26th president of Mexico, he served for well over 10 years and was the first indigenous president of Mexico. The man admired this great leader as he fought for the freedom and independence of his native country. In many ways, he felt that was exactly what he was doing. No longer would foreigners tell his countrymen what to do or how to do it.

He continued north until reaching the town of La Ermita. There he would meet his contact and execute his plan. He liked that term, "execute," for that is what he was about to do. Execute hundreds of Americans across the entire country, all at the same time. A psychological blow that would take many years to come back from. The Americans would be permanently scarred as they were at Pearl Harbor and 9/11. He would have his revenge. He would help to free his country from the Infidels.

He continued north on Francisco Madero. He knew he was getting close and, for the first time, was anxious. Hopefully, his contact was a man of his word. How could he be? He was doing this for money and for money only. Still, if he did as he was told, it would be worth the money. If he failed him, he would die. It would not be pleasant.

He traveled a few kilometers down the road and turned onto the side street that he had been looking for. He drove a short distance and saw that the house was surrounded by a large wall, which had to be at least 12 feet tall. This would ensure privacy and safety. It was hard to tell the size of the house due to the way the walls and trees blocked his view. He pulled into the driveway, knowing that the next phase of the operation was about to start. As he pulled up to the house man in shorts and a dress shirt exited the house and waited for him.

Chapter Two:

The man's name was Mohammad Abu al-Fadi. He was born and raised in Bandar Abbas. A port city in southern Iran. The city was known for trade and commerce. He joined his father's shipping business as a teenager. He quickly learned the business and helped the business grow. As he grew, he noticed his town had also grown. When his father was a young man, the town had only about 12,000 people. It was quiet and peaceful. Now the city boasted almost three-quarters of a million people. It was a fast-paced city with most of the activities near the coast. The growth made the family business grow quickly. His family rose in importance and wealth. With wealth came power, and young Mohammad discovered he liked this power. He liked it a lot.

As a man in his mid-30s, Mohammad ran the family business more and more. His father was proud of the fine son he had raised. His father. Bijan wished his son would marry and give him grandchildren. However, Mohammad had other ideas.

As he became richer and more powerful, he mingled with the political leaders of this country. This was nothing unusual. He was not religious. He did, of course, have to go to certain events to be seen, but this was just in order to instill him in the eyes of other powerful men. He was well-liked by the politicians. Even many of the religious leaders appreciated his donations to the mosques. He enjoyed knowing that he would be seen at the fanciest social gathering and always had a place to pray when he went to the mosque. He always wore the best suits. His Porsche 911 Turbo seemed out of place in the port city. That his car stood out made him feel he was more important than most.

All in all, life was good. He had everything he ever wanted: power, money, and social status, until THAT day. The family shipping business had just purchased a new seagoing freighter. It was 1000 feet long. It fit its name, the Whale. It would be the flagship of the family business. It was a warm spring day when the ship sailed on its first voyage. The trip was more of a shakedown cruise. His father would take the ship out on the maiden voyage to Muscat, in Oman. Then on to Port Said in Egypt. This would require a passage through the Suez Canal, something his father had done many times.

Muscat is a huge city of over 1.5 million people. As the capital and major port of Oman, it had the docks that could accommodate the flagship. The city had been there for almost 2,000 years. It was a pretty city by day or night. Bijan would make a point of attending prayers at the Sultan Qaboos Grand Mosque. This magnificent build could hold over 6,000 worshippers in the main room and 20,000 people at maximum capacity. The dome was over 150 feet high and shone brightly at night. Whenever his father was in Muscat, he would find peace and comfort there.

Although he was scheduled to go with his father on that day, there was trouble at the docks that demanded his immediate attention. A crane had broken, destroying cargo and killing a worker. Three more men had to be taken to the hospital. Mohammad would have to see to medical coverage for his men at the local hospital, trying to salvage the dropped cargo, and of course, replacing the expensive crane as soon as possible. The crane was necessary to continue the loading of his cargo ships. This was the most important duty for him.

Bijan told him not to worry. He had done this trip many times in his life. He had numerous friends and business associates in Muscat. And of course, he wanted to pray in the beautiful Mosque. Mohammad watched the massive ship leave the harbor. He waved at his father on the bridge. He could not see his father, but he knew his father could see him. He loved his father. It would be the last time he ever saw his father.

The huge ship moved slowly out of the harbor. It traveled in a south-east direction. The pilot of the huge ship knew his job and the waters here. He aimed the ship to pass south of Hormoz Island and north of Larak Island. There was lots of room. The ship turned to a more southerly direction into the Strait of Hormuz. With the United Arab Emirates on his right and his home country of Iran on his left, Bijan felt safe and free. The open sea was his home.

It was evening when the big ship docked in Muscat. The ship was tied to the pier, and Bijan walked down the gangplank. He was met by his friend and business associate, Ahmed. They had known each other for years. They were both in the shipping business. However, Ahmed had other business dealings. He was also an arms smuggler. Most of his "products" were sent to the lesser groups in the area. He rarely provided the heavier military weapons, but cases of AK-47s or RPGs would bring in extra income with little extra risk. Today, he had an order for 750 RPGs and various individual weapons to be delivered to "freedom fighters" in Yemen. He was not political. He loved the standard of living these sales allowed him to live.

Ahmed and Bijan embraced, as men do in that part of the world. Ahmed led Bijan to his waiting Mercedes. The big car was kept clean and in perfect order. Ahmed loved the car and the status that it brought. They left the docks and drove along Highway 1 to the west. Ahmed enjoyed the power of the big 8-cylinder engine. He did not care about the price of gasoline or maintenance; this was status. He turned northwest on Al Shati Street. They continued on until they got to the Crowne Plaza Muscat. They pulled into the parking lot and drove up to Ahmed's favorite restaurant. A valet came out to park the Mercedes, but Ahmed waved him off. No one but he would ever drive this car. Not even his sons, as long as he was alive.

He parked the car, and they both got out. The weather was wonderful, warm, and a breeze from the water. They entered the restaurant and sat outside so they could see the water. Both men loved the water. The scenery was beautiful. Ahmed ordered the salmon, and Bijan ordered the steamed seafood platter. They drank iced water. Both were Muslims and would not drink alcohol. They ate for a while and talked about their families and businesses.

Ahmed turned to his friend and asked, "I have a favor to ask you, sort of a business deal."

"Of course, my friend, what is it?" replied Bijan.

"I understand you are going to Port Said."

Bijan nodded, but was a bit concerned about how his friend knew his final destination. After all, he had called Ahmed just that morning and told him about stopping in Muscat. He never mentioned his final destination.

"What is it I can do for you, my old friend?"

Ahmed leaned back in his chair and smiled. "One of my customers has asked for a delivery of machine parts as soon as possible to Al Hudaydah. He said it is of the utmost urgency and is willing to pay extras for a rapid delivery."

Bijan knew this was not unusual; businesses had more money than they could spend. However, if the machinery that supplied oil or water broke, it was always considered a crisis.

"Of course, my old friend, but there is a problem. This is our first cruise, and I only have enough people to operate the ship and not enough to load and secure heavy equipment."

"That will not be a problem," smiled Ahmed. "My people will load and unload the crates. I would not ask you to do that work." "Of course, I hope you will let them sail with you. I will cover all expenses and compensate you for any problems this might cause."

"That is not necessary, I am going that way."

Ahmed smiled and said, "Let me at least buy this dinner." Bijan raised his glass of ice water and agreed. After dinner, they went to Ahmed's home. It was huge. They sat and talked about old times for a while, and then Bijan excused himself. It had been a long day, and he would have to get up early in the morning to ensure his ship was ready. He went to the guest room, where he took a long, hot bath and then slept a dreamless sleep. He woke at 5 AM, dressed, and went to have breakfast with his old friend. He did not know this would be his last breakfast.

Ahmed drove Bijan to the port. It was a quiet, uneventful drive. Bijan thought that Ahmed drove his Mercedes too fast, but such is the way of things. They arrived and parked near the pier office. Ahmed had a reserve parking place. Another sign of wealth, power, and influence.

As Bijan approached his ship, he observed a group of men moving several large crates onto his ship. There was something wrong. They worked very slowly compared to a normal dock crew. They did not seem familiar with the cranes and hoists normally found at any dock.

Ahmed approached Bijan and noticed how Bijan was studying the workers. Ahmed apologized, "I am so sorry. This is not a regular crew. I had to hire these men because of the rush order. My regular workers are all committed to other tasks right now. They will stay with the cargo until it is unloaded. Maybe they can learn something on this trip to make them better workers."

Bijan agreed, after all this time, Ahmed had been a friend for many years. How bad could the workers be? They loaded several large wooden crates on the ship. They did not seem as heavy as the crates normally used to carry the huge pumps, which were normally transported in this part of the world. Whether it was oil or water, huge amounts of liquid had to be pumped daily in the Middle East.

After a while, the ship's captain signaled Bijan that they were ready to sail. Bijan and Ahmed embraced, shook hands, and said their goodbyes. Bijan invited Ahmed to visit him at his home in Iran. There they would have a good dinner and discuss old times. Bijan boarded his ship. He gave the captain the approval to get on the way. The lines holding the ship to the shore were released and pulled back onto the ship. The gangplank was also retracted. Harbor tugs help to move the ship away from the pier and out into open water.

Bijan, who normally watched these operations but never got into the captain's business, observed Ahmed's workers. They seemed not to know what they were doing. Actually, they were not doing anything to help with the shipboard activities. Some of them just walked around the deck. Others just sat next to the wood crates. It was as if they were guarding them. This seemed foolish. The ship was at sea, and these "workers" and the cargo were here with the blessing of the ship's owner. Everything was perfectly safe. Bijan would have fun kidding Ahmed about the quality of the workers he hired. Bijan would never allow that caliber of workers on his ships.

The ship turned southeast and sailed along the Oman coast. The water was beautiful, and the air was clear. Perfect weather for the trip. The ship's captain would inspect every operation and piece of equipment. He was a true professional. The ship would turn southwest and sail past Oman's southern coast and then the waters of Yemen. Later, the ship would turn northwest along the Yemeni coast and head for the waters between Saudi Arabia and Sudan. Yes, it would be an easy voyage through known waters.

Chapter Three

The U.S.S Stephen Casey is an Arleigh Burke-class destroyer. She, ships are always referred to as "she," was the newest version of a class of ships that had been the pride of the U S Navy since 1989. She was named after a Navy Corpsman who heroically gave his life saving the lives of several Marines. Casey was a corpsman, a medic, who traveled with U. S. Marines. Marines do not have their own medics and rely on the Navy for that service. Casey and "his Marines" walked into an ambush. The explosive blast, which triggered the attack, killed several Marines. A few managed to get themselves out of the kill zone. There were four badly wounded Marines who could not get out of the kill zone. Petty Officer Casey ran through enemy machine gun and rifle fire to reach Corporal Jackson. Casey picked the huge man up, put him over his shoulder, and ran through enemy fire again to carry Jackson to safety. Once Jackson was stabilized, Casey ran back through the enemy fire to save Sergeant McNeil. Once again, carrying the wounded Marine to safety. For his efforts, Casey took a bullet in the leg and shrapnel in his arms and back. Casey refused to quit. For a third time, he ran into the gun battle to get to Lance Corporal Bergman. Bergman had been shot in both legs. Casey carried him to safety. Casey's running had been slowed by exhaustion and loss of blood. He was shot in his side; shrapnel cut his face and neck. After carrying Bergman to safety, Casey collapsed. He was exhausted and covered in blood, both his own and that of the wounded Marines. As he lay on the filthy street, he heard his name being called. Lieutenant Anderson lay in the rubble. The lieutenant's uniform was covered in blood. Casey knew he could not leave a Marine behind. As he started his fourth run, his luck ran out. The bullet went through his chest and burned like fire. He fell. He thought about his wife and young son. He thought about the lieutenant and his family. With superhuman effort, Casey ignored the pain. He ignored the blood loss. He tried to stand, but fell again. He refused to let the lieutenant die. He dragged himself across the kill zone. Marines opened fire with devastating accuracy on the enemy. Some died, some were wounded, and some hid. Casey had crawled to the wounded officer. Unable to stand, let alone carry Anderson, Casey got his arm into the lieutenant's web gear. Casey then crawled across the kill zone one last time, dragging the officer behind him. Every breath burned, every part of his body was on fire. He crawled on. Even with the Marines laying down fire, a few of the enemy managed to get a few shots off. Another bullet hit Casey in the back. The pain was beyond belief. Casey finished his crawl for life. The lieutenant was treated by the other Marines and another corpsman who had just arrived with reinforcements. All four wounded Marines would live. Petty Officer Casey would not.

He was awarded America's highest award for his selfless act. A ship was named in his honor. Navy Commander Joshua Lawrence knew this story well. He was the commanding officer of the U.S.S. Casey, the captain of the ship. He knew this story. When he was a

Midshipman at the Naval Academy, this ship was barely in the design phase. The Arleigh Burke class destroyers had been modernized several times. Newer radar, better weapons, and worldwide communications systems. During his career, he has served on a variety of ships and in a variety of roles. Some were minor roles, and others were career-building. He never let a "lesser" assignment get him down. He gave 110% all the time. He was the honor graduate at the Surface Warfare Officer's course. This was held in Newport, Rhode Island, over 5 months of intense training. His last assignment was as the executive officer (XO) of a different destroyer. His commanding officer recommended him for promotion to full commander and the captaincy of his own ship. It was the proudest moment of his life.

With the name of a hero who gave it his all as the name of his ship, he knew he was in the right place. He knew this ship from bow to stern. All 509 feet of her. Her weapons systems and her limitations. He also knew the name of every person on his ship. He could recognize every one of them. This took a little time as there were over 300 sailors on his ship. This is how to lead.

The Casey was at sea near Al Hudaydah. With about three-quarters of a million people, it was the fourth-largest city in Yemen. This area is north of where the Gulf of Aden meets the Red Sea. It is a major shipping route not just for oil but for a vast array of supplies going toward Suez. The Casey was on patrol to ensure international shipping was not subject to piracy and that international narcotics and weapons smuggling was not allowed.

Lawrence was on the bridge. The skies were clear, the sea as calm. His ship was making about 8 knots (about 10mph) while patrolling his assigned sector. There were several ships proceeding through the area. All were properly registered, and with no intelligence about illegal activities, they proceeded on their way without incident. It was a day like most days here. All that was about to change.

Chapter Four

His name was Brian Maxwell. Or at least, that was the name he went by. Maxwell had been working in the US Embassy in Muscat for over six years. It was not a secret that he was not really a cultural attaché. Everyone knew that Maxwell was actually a representative Central Intelligence Agency. His job was not glamorous like that of movie spies. He basically kept an ear out for what was going on in the country and, on occasion, would pick up little tidbits of information from the past back to his headquarters in Virginia. After six years of service, he had never scored a major intelligence victory. He provided translations of local newspapers and reported on events occurring in the area that he felt would be of interest.

He had made many contacts over his time in Muscat. Some were small shop owners, some were executives of large corporations. They all knew who he was and what he represented. Different people have different motivations for providing information. Sometimes one rival group would inform another rival, hoping that there would be some type of official intervention, and thereby reduce the competition. He learned to speak the language and observe local customs. This made him less offensive as a foreigner to local residents.

He liked his small office in the Embassy. It was plain and unassuming. The most important part was his view of the sea. Some reason he could sit and watch the water for hours. It helped him relax. When he was conducting his business in the office, the specially designed window shutters closed over the windows. This kept not only prying eyes out of his office, but also kept sophisticated listening devices from penetrating his office.

He thought it was going to be just another day. He had no idea that what happened today would set off the largest terrorist event in the history of the United States. He was just doing his job, and there was no way he could foresee what was about to happen.

He received a phone call from one of his reliable sources. The source told him of some strange activity at the docks. He could come to the dock and see for himself. He said it was something special only asked for 50 Rials for the information. Maxwell had gotten reliable information before from this source. He told the source he would come to the docks and see for himself. If the information was good, 50 Rials would be paid out immediately.

He did not like sitting in the office all day, and a trip to the docks would give him an excuse to leave the Embassy. It was a short walk to the pier. He took his time and walked slowly, observing the shops and the people on the streets. One never knew when something of interest would make itself known.

They met at a small café near the pier. He ordered 2 cups of strong black coffee, which, of course, he paid for. After a few moments of pleasant conversation and making sure they were not being observed, the informant started.

"Do you see the large cargo ship that left, which is flying the Iranian flag?" "It is a new ship that has never docked here before." Maxwell was starting to get a bit impatient. Cargo ships were always arriving in Muscat. Cargo ships arrive many times every day. There was nothing unusual here.

"So, what makes this ship so special that it's worth the money you've asked for?" The informant smiled. He was saving the best for last. He enjoyed watching Maxwell get impatient with. It was a game they played.

"It is not the ship that is important; it is the new cargo taken on board in the port."

"Do you know of Ahmed, who owns several ships in this area?" Maxwell fought to himself, of course, I do. He uses the shipping industry for smuggling. While Maxwell never could prove this, he knew that Ahmed shipped anything, for anyone, if the price was right.

After finishing the coffee, Maxwell paid the bill and left a decent tip. He did not want to appear to be cheap nor extravagant. Just an average person blending into the business area. The informant led Maxwell office building situated nearby. They took the elevator to the top floor and then the emergency stairs to the roof, where they could look down and see the deck of the Iranian ship. The informant advised Maxwell that the large wooden crates on the deck of the ship were placed there yesterday by workers who worked for Ahmed. The creates were not on any manifest, and the workers were not part of any working group on the docks. Maxwell asked what was in the crates. The informant did not know, but it was strange that the crew who loaded the crates stayed with them all night. These workers stayed awake all night, surrounding the crates. It seemed that they were guarding them. Maxwell was now interested. There was no way he could get on the ship. Even if he did, he could not get past the guards. He had no authority to inspect the ship. He knew of Ahmed and knew he would be of little or no help. Asking questions would alert Ahmed. Maxwell paid the informant and then went directly to his office. He wrote up an intelligence summary and sent it to CIA headquarters. Maybe they had more pieces of the puzzle.

The analyst at the CIA got the report a few hours later. She had heard chatter that Ahmed was supporting terrorist groups, for a price. Her interest was keyed. With her boss's permission, she called the United States Central Command in Tampa, Florida. She knew she had to go through channels, even if it slowed the transmission. She contacted Navy Captain Joe Briggs. He was high enough in the intelligence staff at CENTCOM to make things happen. He thanked her and sent a flash message to United States Naval Forces Central Command in Bahrain. They would do the follow-up and see what, if anything, was going on.

Chapter Five

"Captain on the bridge," shouted the boatswain's mate.

Lawrence smiled to himself. The captain of a Navy ship was a major career assignment. It could make or break a promising career. Just being selected to command was a major feat. Experience, education, and past performance were some of the factors considered by the command selection board. Competition was fierce. There were only so many ships to command. Then again, there were difference types of ships. Aircraft careers were usually commanded by aviators with experience in both flying and leadership. Submarines are only commanded by submarine-qualified officers. However, there is more to the story. The officers who ranked the highest might get a cruiser or a destroyer. Front-line combat ships. The Navy had dozens of less glamorous ships. All critically important, but not as career-enhancing. Someone had to bring fuel, ammunition, and mail to the ships at sea. An aircraft carrier with 6,000 people needed a lot of food on a regular basis. Someone needed to command those ships.

On his ship, the captain was the ultimate authority. Army, Marine, or Air Force officers of the same rank and in command had much less power over their people and equipment. The captain was responsible for everything the ship and all his personnel did or did not do. Awake or asleep, it made no difference; the captain was responsible. He remembered studying the career of a famous naval officer. As a new junior officer, he was standing the watch when the ship ran aground on a sandbar that was not on the charts. He faced a military tribunal for "hazarding the ship." This is a major sin in the Navy. He thought his career was over until a senior officer stepped in and, seeing potential in the young officer, gave him a second chance. Chester Nimitz retired as one of only a few 5-star admiral ever to serve in the Navy. Lawrence knew that type of generosity would be extremely rare in today's Navy.

His second in command, his executive officer or XO, was a very sharp lieutenant commander named Hector Sanchez. Sanchez got his commission through Navy ROTC. He was the number one student in his graduating class. More importantly, Sanchez had spent his entire career on destroyers. He had every possible job, except captain. He knew the ship's systems as well as, or maybe better than, the specialists who operated the systems. Lawrence knew he was lucky to have such a qualified officer as his XO. He also knew that Sanchez would someday command his own ship. Lawrence had a good ship and a good crew.

The ship's current mission was to patrol the Red Sea. They covered the area between Yemen and Eritrea. They were there to protect international commerce vessels from pirates. Yes, pirates, in this day and age. This area of the world was full of cargo ships carrying goods all over the Middle East and on to Europe. While these ships and their cargo were worth hundreds of millions of dollars, they were unarmed. Their corporations would not let these ships fight back. A few pirates in a speed boat, armed only with rifles and maybe a few rocket-propelled grenades, could capture a 1,000-foot-long ship and ransom it for millions. The American Navy was in the area trying to stop these thieves and keep commerce alive in the region. Generally, the sight of the warship was enough to make the pirates think twice. If they did not fire on a ship, the Navy would not fire on them.

This was the second month of a four-month "cruise." Cruise sounded better than a deployment, like the other services call their overseas assignments. Their ship had most of the comforts of being at a base. The food was excellent, there was a library, internet access for studying and writing home. They could even video conference with their families at home. Seeing loved ones was a great morale boost.

Everything was going well, and Lawrence, seated in his captain's chair, was just starting to relax when Chief Jackson, from the CIC, entered the bridge. The CIC, or combat information center, was the tactical hub for the ship. Intelligence was received and analyzed. Information from the ship's various electronic systems came here to be reviewed by intelligence specialists. Communications from higher and adjacent ships and organizations were examined here.

"What is it chief?" Lawrence asked.

The chief usually stayed in the CIC. "Skipper, we just got an alert from CENTCOM," and handed Lawrence a sheet of paper.

The captain read the paper carefully. "How solid is this, chief?"

Jackson thought for a moment. "Skipper, this was bounced from those civilian folks to CENTCOM with flash priority."

Lawrence knew "those civilian folks" were the CIA. They mean well, but do not always get it right. They are limited in the quality of their informants. Human intelligence was not like the movies.

"So, we are supposed to find this Iranian freighter and see if it is acting suspiciously?

"Sir," the chief replied, "They are tracking it using both SIGINT and IMINT; they must think there is something to it, to use all those assets."

Lawrence knew that SIGINT, or signal intelligence, could monitor radio or even phone communications. Nothing said without encryption was safe. IMINT or image intelligence, usually referred to aerial photography made by planes, drones, or satellites. All their information was usually Top Secret or above. While the information might be shared, the source of it rarely was. Just didn't need to know.

"OK, chief, where is she now?"

"She is headed this way, just passing Mocha, making about 6 knots."

"So, about 100 miles or so?" asked Lawrence. "I do not want this encounter to be conducted at night." Lawrence thought a moment and then ordered come right to course 150, all ahead standard." The ship responded, turning to the right and picking up speed.

"Chief, keep me updated on that ship's course and speed."

"Aye aye" was the response from the chief.

He sat in the captain's chair and thought. He had a ship that could take down several warships at one time. It could shoot down jet aircraft and defend itself from drones and enemy missiles. But what were the Rules of Engagement for stopping a civilian cargo ship? Based on the limited intelligence he had, the ship had broken no laws, and its crew, or at least part of its crew, was acting suspiciously. "What the heck does that mean"? He thought to himself. He could signal them to stop using either signal flags or lamps. Suppose they didn't stop? Then what? He was not going to sink a cargo ship for not stopping, not based on this limited intelligence. He could fire a shot across her bow. So, he was shooting at an unarmed ship; no, he needed clarification.

"XO, I'll be in my quarters for a few."

The XO moved immediately to the center of the bridge and took command of the ship's operation. He would not sit in the captain's chair out of respect.

Lawrence checked his orders for this mission. Reading the Rules of Engagement twice, he still was not sure. If a ship attacked any other ship or land target, he could fire on it. If the ship posed an immediate threat to his ship, he had a duty to protect it. But this? He had a very fine line to thread. Maybe he could use this as a training situation. His crew could always use realistic training in decision-making under stress. He would see how good his XO really was.

He returned to the bridge. "Captain is on the bridge," someone shouted. "XO, how is it going?"

"Fine, Sir," said the young lieutenant commander.

"How long before we encounter this mystery ship?"

"Mystery ship?" said the XO.

"Yes, it is a mystery why they want us to stop it." They both smiled.

"Still nothing on the radar. Intelligence updates say we should make contact with her in about two hours."

"XO, I have a mission for you. You will prepare two response teams. One if they are peaceful, one if they are not. Keep the armed team out of sight; we do not want to provoke a response. Board her, inspect her, and then let us get out of here."

Lawrence had had bad experiences with faulty intelligence in the past. The analysts meant well, but guessing with limited information can be tricky. He did not want an international incident or worse on his watch. This ship, the Whale, could be anything or nothing, and Lawrence did not want to bother some honest businessman and his crew for this kind of report.

Chapter Six

It was late afternoon, and Bijan stood on the bridge of his ship. The weather was wonderful. The breeze was refreshing. He had made this trip many times, but always enjoyed seeing the land from the sea. Watching the small towns on the banks of the sea grow over time. He felt right at home. He was still concerned about Ahmed's crew. They just sat around the crates and did nothing. Even at meal time, some of them stayed with the crates. They even slept in shifts. Bijan could not understand their action concerning some machinery. This type of cargo travelled in these waters every day. He would definitely need to talk to Ahmed when he got back from this trip.

"Captain, CIC reports the vehicle is now on radar."

"Very well," replied Lawrence. "XO, what is your plan?"

Sanchez looked his boss in the eye and advised, "I have two teams. One will only have side arms. They will accompany me for the inspection. The other teams will have full tactical gear and both side arms and rifles. They will be led by the Master at Arms."

The Master at Arms was usually a senior noncommissioned officer responsible for security and law enforcement on the ship. They received training over and above the other sailors in these fields.

"I would also request we launch our copter. The Seahawk could provide a better view of their activities and would show our resolve."

Lawrence considered this and asked, "Do you want the ship at Battle Stations?"

"No," said the XO. Battle stations would require every sailor, on or off duty, to man their station. While important, this type of response was unnecessarily taxing on the crew.

Lawrence said he concurred. "Good plan, XO, it's all yours."

While the XO was assembling these teams, the Seahawk helicopter took off. Destroyer captains of WWII and Korea would be jealous to have their own air assets. But this was the 21st century, and aircraft were considered an integral part of any military operation. The helicopter would cruise at 5 times the speed of the destroyer to get to the target. It could go much faster, if needed. The Seahawk was about 65 feet long and had a range of over 400 miles, or 380 nautical miles, as the measurement the Navy used.

On board The Whale, everything was calm until the Seahawk flew by. It was totally normal for folks on ships to look up at a low-flying aircraft. As the Seahawk slowed to get a better look at the ship, Lieutenant Sarah Hawkins, the pilot of the Seahawk, observed several men running around the deck and hiding behind several large crates. Hiding from a helicopter on an open deck made no sense to her. She slowed the helicopter down to match the speed of the cargo ship. What she saw made no sense. Two or three people on the bridge waved at her, but the deck crew looked like it was trying to open the crates. She wondered what the cargo might be. She had no idea.

Hawkins contacted the Casey. "Dolphin 6-1, this is Egert 1-1."

"Go ahead 1-1," came the instant response.

"Be advised, there is something wrong here. Crew racing around deck, trying to open crates on deck."

"1-1, this is 6-1, shadow ship until we make contact. Do not engage or press them."

"Roger," said Hawkins. She wondered what the heck was going on.

Commander Lawrence had the same thoughts. First, the CIA says there is something going on, and now their actions heighten his concern. He advised the XO of the report. Sanchez, who had never fired a shot in anger, worried that would all change today.

Bijan and the ship's captain were not concerned. He had seen or heard about so many flyovers by the American Navy. He had no love for America, but they never bothered him. He was not a religious zealot who believed it was his duty to attack Americans whenever he could. They could fly around, and he would continue on their trip. He was concerned about the workers on the deck. They were acting most strangely. Trying to hide from a helicopter on the deck of a flat ship seemed foolish. What really concerned him was their attempt to open the crates that his friend Ahmed asked him to transport. He got a chill and wondered if there were drugs or weapons in the crates. Those were the normal illegal cargo in the area. It could not be drugs; the crates were too large. Still, one never knows. One of the workers was running across the deck and heading for the bridge. Maybe he could get some answers now.

The man ran up the stairs to the bridge and burst through the door. "You must speed up and get away from the helicopter. It will bring navy ships."

Bijan did not take orders from deckhands on his own ship. "Who are you and what is this about? he demanded.

"Who am I? I am the man with the gun," as he pulled some type of black pistol from under his shirt. Bijan did not know about guns, but he was sure it could kill him. "Your boss, Ahmed, asked me for a favor, and this is how I am treated, on my own ship?"

Bijan could hear the rage in his voice, but he didn't care. The rumors about Ahmed must be true. He was a smuggler. "Even if I wanted to, we can not outrun the helicopter. We are fairly empty and could probably make 25 knots; the helicopter can make 5 or 6 times that speed. There is nowhere to run." Bijan could see the panic in the man's eyes. "What is in those crates? What is making you so nervous?"

"None of your business," came the reply.

"Those crates are on my ship, so it is my business. Maybe I should look for myself."

The man raised the pistol and pointed it at Bijan. "If you leave the bridge, I will shoot you. If you do not go full speed, I will shoot the captain." Bijan knew he had no leverage.

He looked at the captain, saying, "All ahead full."

The helicopter noticed the speed change and radioed the Casey immediately. Lawrence was now very concerned. He knew something was going on, but had no idea what. The Casey would intercept The Whale within the next 5 minutes.

Hawkins radioed that she was going to take a closer look. She slowed the helicopter to match the speed of The Whale. The ship was increasing her speed, but matching it was no problem for the skilled aviator. The Navy had high standards for its pilots, and Hawkins was darn good. She was a bit disappointed when she was assigned to helicopters and not jets. She could do things with a helicopter that few could. Her recommendation for the transition to jets was working its way up the chain of command. She knew Lawrence had written her an exceptional review.

As she maneuvered closer to the large ship, she could clearly see several men forcing open several crates with hand tools. She knew something was going on. These men look frantic, but she didn't know why. She hit the intercom button and told the sailor seated behind her to ready his weapon, but not to fire or even display it without orders.

Even though she used the intercom, she turned slightly to look at the sailor she was speaking to. As she looked back at the ship, she saw several men on the deck who were now armed with some type of assault rifle. Her skills paid off as she made the helicopter quickly climb and move away from the freighter. Several men pointed their weapons at her, but did not fire. She was already out of range.

"6-1, this is 1-1, over," she said into her helmet microphone.

"6-1 over" came the response immediately. "I need 6-1 actual," she said, asking for the captain and not the bridge officer. Within a minute came the response,

"This is 6-1 actual, what's going on?" said Lawrence.

"This is 1-1; the ship has accelerated away from me. Workers have opened several deck crates and displayed some kind of automatic rifle. No shots were fired, but they pointed the weapons at us. I put some distance between us."

"Did you fire?" asked Lawrence.

"Negative, no shots fired."

"Good job," said Lawrence. "Keep them in sight, report activity, but stay out of weapons' range. We will be there in a couple of minutes."

Lawrence turned to the XO and could see that he heard the conversation. "Well, XO, this just got a lot more interesting." Sanchez said, "I want all sailors going with me on the boarding party to have full battle dress, not just the second team." Lawrence nodded, and Sanchez ordered the first team to get into full gear and get back ASAP. The Casey bridge crew could see "The Whale" in the distance. That distance was closing quickly. The Seahawk could also be seen. Lawrence ordered the speed to be reduced to 1/3. 500 feet of ship slowed. The sea churned on either side of them. The XO was on the port side of the deck. He was also wearing tactical gear. He was armed with only a pistol, a 9mm. He, like all the other men, wore helmets. They knew something was going to happen. They did not know what.

Lawrence could see the open crates on the deck of The Whale. Even with his binoculars, it was hard to tell what was or what had been in the crates. "Signal them who we are and to stop their vessel. Prepare to be boarded," commanded Lawrence. While the signal man flashed the message with the standard signal lamp, radio men attempted to contact the ship by radio. They tried in English. A junior female radio operator spoke in Farsi. There was no response from the Whale. She was at full speed. Boarding her would be impossible.

The man on the bridge of the Whale kept his pistol pointed at the ship's captain. "Do not stop, do not slow down, or you both die." Bijan did not know what to do. This had never happened to him. Being hijacked on his own ship. Sure, he had heard of these things happening, but not to him. There would be hell to pay when he saw Ahmed next. If he ever saw Ahmed again.

He shouted at the hijacker, "We cannot outrun or outfight the Navy ship. Let us stop and see what they want."

The hijacker laughed. "They want the cargo."

"How could they want the cargo?" Even Bijan did not know what it was. Bijan could clearly see the destroyer now. He could see a dozen or so sailors on the deck. They appeared to be armed with rifles of some kind. Bijan said a silent prayer to his God.

Lawrence knew this encounter was going downhill very fast. He could not board her at that speed, and something must be going on for them to take rifles and point them at his helicopter.

"1-1. This is 6-1, what do you see on the ship?"

Hawkins came back immediately. "At least 10 men, 7 have rifles, and the other 3 are opening another crate."

"Take up a position on their starboard side, but not too close. We will pass by their port side." They can't be stupid enough to fire on us, thought Lawrence.

"Keep going straight, at full speed," demanded the gunman on the bridge.

"We can't do this," said Bijan. "It is madness."

"We make it through, or we die. A glorious martyr's death." Bijan could see the destroyer clearly now. Sailors with weapons on one side of his ship and that helicopter on the other. Where could he go, what could he do? The man on the bridge yelled something to the men on the deck. Bijan thought it was odd because he spoke several languages. Several of the men on the deck moved to the port side with their weapons. Three others finished opening the crate. They removed three RPG launchers and readied them for firing.

Hawkins yelled on the radio, "RPGs," and banked right to increase the range between her and the cargo ship. One of the men on the deck raised the launcher, aimed, and fired at the helicopter. RPGs do not have a guidance system. You aim, you fire, sort of like firing a rifle, but with much bigger and slower bullets. Seaman Darcy, seated in the cargo area of the helicopter, saw the launch and the streak coming towards him.

"Incoming," he yelled. Hawkins was already taking evasive maneuvers. She dove the helicopter to the right. By diving and not trying to climb, she increased her speed quickly. She and Darcy saw the RPG fly past them and continue to climb. The RPG ran out of fuel and crashed harmlessly into the sea.

"6-1, this is 1-1, took an RPG round, it missed, we are OK," Hawkins reported instantly over the radio.

On board the Casey, Sanchez heard the radio message. He instantly ordered the sailors to load their weapons and take cover, if they could. Sanchez then looked to Lawrence. Lawrence nodded his head. He had a good XO. Lawrence then turned to Lieutenant Edmonds, "Weapons officer, track that ship and be prepared to engage with the deck gun. The deck gun, located on the front deck, was a Mark 45 5-inch gun. It could be used against surface, land, or aerial targets. The weapon could fire 16 – 20 rounds a minute. Each round fired weighed almost 70 pounds. It was a very versatile and effective weapon. Edmonds had fired the big gun on a test range. He was qualified with the weapon and knew its power. He had never fired at a living thing.

Lawrence ordered his communications people to continue to try to contact "the Whale." He knew they would not answer, but this was proper procedure, and he was hoping to avoid an all-out fight. He knew his ship could do the job, but he did not want to blow up a civilian ship without making every attempt to avoid it. Firing an RPG at Hawkins told him this would not go well.

"Slow to one third," he ordered. The two ships would pass each other. Their port sides facing each other. The Whale continued towards them at full speed. Lawrence remembered the famous quote of Lord Horatio Nelson, probably the most famous English Admiral, "No captain can do very wrong if he places his ship alongside that of the enemy." Lawrence sure hoped the admiral was right.

As the two ships passed each other, nothing happened. His sailors on the deck had their weapons ready but held their fire. Lawrence could see the men on the deck of the cargo ship. Some had rifles, others had RPG launchers; they held their fire. Maybe, just maybe, Lawrence prayed. The bow of the Casey was almost even with the stern of the Whale when all hell broke loose.

Lawrence watched as a man on the walkway outside the bridge started screaming at the men on the deck. Lawrence did not understand a single word, but the intent was obvious. At least a half dozen men on the Whale opened fire with some type of shoulder-fired automatic weapon. Lawrence had a slight knowledge of these types of weapons. A ship's captain rarely encountered these weapons at sea. Two RPGs were also fired at his ship. Lawrence could see them streaking towards his ship. He turned to see that Sanchez had already ordered the sailors to return fire.

The RPGs slammed into the bridge area. The concussion stunned everyone. Several crew members were on the floor, bleeding. At least two were obviously dead. There were several small fires, and there were electrical wires hanging from the ceiling.

Lawrence commanded, "General quarters, weapons officer, engage that ship."

The klaxon sounded, and every member of the crew, whether on or off duty, ran to their battle stations. Firefighters put on their protective gear. Others grabbed their helmets and vests. It looked like chaos, but it was a well-rehearsed drill the crew had practiced many times. Within a few minutes, every crew member was ready for the war they had just entered.

Lieutenant Edmonds tried to turn the 5-inch gun on the Whale. He knew they were too close for a missile attack. Unlike ships a generation older, the Casey did not have large weapons positioned around the ship. The 5-inch was located at the bow area. It could traverse 170 degrees to either side. While not ideal, Edmonds turned the weapon to the extreme left.

On the port side, Sanchez and his teams were engaging the men on the deck of the Whale. As soon as the first RPG was fired, Sanchez ordered the sailors to open fire. His men laid down a barrage of 5.56 mm ammo. Many of the enemy were dropped where they stood. One of Sanchez's men, Machinist Mate 2nd class Jackson, was hit by small arms fire coming from the Whale. Jackson dropped to the deck, bleeding from two bullets that hit him in the stomach area. Sanchez, seeing this, left his position behind a steel plate and ran through enemy fire to Jackson.

"Hold on, Jackson, I've got you," yelled Sanchez over the weapons fire. Sanchez grabbed Jackson by the vest and dragged him to a place of relative safety. That is when he heard the explosion.

It wasn't exactly an explosion, as it was the muzzle blast of the 5-inch gun being fired by Edmonds. The gun was pointed almost in their direction. The shells whistled past en route to the bridge of the Whale. The three-round burst hit the bridge with devastating effect. The bridge exploded, sending pieces of metal and glass in all directions. Bijan, his ship's captain and the leader of the deck crew, disappeared into a mist. There would be no bodies to bury. Edmonds fired another 3-round burst into the superstructure of the vessel. This was an unarmored vessel. It was not designed to withstand naval gunfire.

"Cease Fire," ordered Lawrence. The cargo ship was burning; there were numerous bodies on the deck. The firing had stopped, and the ship was slowing. "Status report," demanded Lawrence.

There were two dead sailors on the bridge where the RPGs struck. Designed to take out a tank or a bunker, the strong glass windows around the bridge could not absorb the blasts. There were three injured sailors on the bridge. Navy Corpsmen rushed to the bridge, stabilized their wounds, and carried them to the ship's sick bay. Lieutenant Commander Sanchez picked up Jackson and carried him to sick bay for medical attention. There was no time to wait for the corpsmen to get to him. Jackson needed help now. Other sailors helped Sanchez navigate the passageways and carry Jackson. Once Jackson made it to the sick bay, Sanchez raced to the bridge. He knew it had been hit by two RPGs. He did not know if Lawrence was still alive. If Lawrence were dead or wounded, he would have to take command of the ship. He hoped he was ready for that responsibility.

Sanchez entered the bridge and observed the destruction. He had never seen anything like this. There was a lot of blood on the floor. There were a lot fewer people here than there should have been. Lawrence saw Sanchez and was relieved that he was okay. Then he saw Sanchez's shirt, arms, and face covered in blood.

"My God, are you alright?" asked Lawrence. He was still looking at Snachez and seeing blood everywhere.

"I am fine," said Sanchez. " It is not my blood. I carried Jackson to sick bay; he was hit twice."

Both men breathed a bit easier. They looked out of the hole that used to be a window. The Whale had stopped dead in the water. There were numerous fires on her deck. There were also some minor explosions going off.

"I wonder what that is?" Sanchez asked.

"If you are up to it, take a team over there and find out. I want to know what the hell is going on." "While the ship is moved closer to the Whale, I have a radio message to send. We will need more medical help."

Just then, the Chief of the Boat, or COB, the senior enlisted sailor on the ship, walked up to Lawrence. "Captain, we have two dead, six wounded, some critical."

Lawrence could feel the blood drain from his face. "Other than the damage to the bridge, the ship is fine. Most of their bullets just bounced off the hull. We will need a little paint."

"Thank you, COB," said Lawrence. "Make sure our wounded get the best possible treatment and our dead are treated with respect."

"Already done, Skipper," said the COB. He was a true professional. He had spent almost his entire career of 22 years at sea and could probably do every job on the ship, except the electronic signal intelligence work. He was a boat driver, not a spy.

Lawrence took a breath. The entire event took only a few minutes. He was emotionally exhausted. He had dead and wounded sailors, damage to this ship, and a burning civilian cargo ship. This will make for a hell of a report. "I'll be in my cabin, get me NAVCENT on the horn." NAVCENT was the naval component of the United States Central Command [CENTCOM]. CENTCOM was the headquarters for all US military operations that cover the area from Egypt to Kazakhstan, about 4 million square miles, and about half a billion people. To most people, it was just the "Middle East." Arguably, the moist violate area in the world.

Lawrence composed himself and picked up the phone in his cabin, a small room off the bridge. "This is Commander Lawrence, the captain of the USS Casey. Please put on the senior duty officer."

"Standby," came the response.

A minute later, a much older voice came on the line. "This is Captain Stanford, senior duty officer."

Lawrence spent the next few minutes explaining his mission and what happened. He also requested advanced medical aid for his wounded. He advised that his personnel were about to board the

Whale. They would document everything they found and photograph it.

"Very well," said Stanford. "If you can stabilize your wounded, get them on a Seahawk to Hodeidah International Airport. I'll get a plane there to transport them to the nearest US hospital that can handle their wounds." "Is your ship seaworthy?" asked Stanford.

"Yes, sir. All systems are working, but we will need some repairs and paint." Stanford smiled to himself. A sense of humor in the face of all this was a good sign.

"Very well, Lawrence. Keep me updated as soon as possible. I will have someone here dedicated to you and your ship."

Lawrence directed Hawkins to land back on the destroyer. He met her on the flight deck. "I have two missions for you. One, take the XO and a landing party to that cargo ship. As soon as you are done, refuel and take our wounded to Hodeidah International Airport. CENTCOM will have an aircraft there to take them to a hospital. I want you ready to go now."

"I am ready for the landing party now, but I should get some more fuel before I head to the airport," Hawkins said.

Just then, Sanchez and four other sailors appeared on the flight deck and headed for the Seahawk.

"I will have the refueling ready for you as soon as you are back. We will bring up the wounded now," said Lawrence.

Sanchez and his team boarded the Seahawk. Hawkins lifted off. It would only take a minute or so to get the XO and the team onto the cargo ship. As soon as she touched down on the cargo ship, Sanchez and his team leaped from the helicopter. Hawkins flew directly back to the Casey. She could see the refueling equipment ready for her. She landed, and the refueling process was immediately started. Lawrence, the COB, and others help to carry the three most badly injured to the bird. A corpsman also boarded to provide medical care on the flight.

"Get them to the airport ASAP," yelled Lawrence over the rotor noise. She jumped back into the pilot's seat.

Lawrence gave her a thumbs-up signifying that the wounded crew members were secured in the helicopter. Her copilot, Lieutenant (J.G.) Herman had already plotted the course to the airport. She made sure Darcy had secured the side door, and she lifted off. The weather was excellent, and she would push the Seahawk as much as possible to get their shipmates to the airport and advanced medical care as quickly as possible. Once these sailors were on an aircraft to a hospital somewhere, she would refuel and head back to the Casey.

Back on the Whale, Sanchez and his team surveyed the ship. There were a few deckhands still alive, but they seemed to be part of the normal crew. They had been below when the shooting had started. One spoke limited English. He stated that he was part of the regular crew, as were these others. Sanchez eyes them suspiciously. He stated that this was a shakedown voyage for the Whale. The captain and owner of the shipping line were being held at gunpoint on the bridge. Sanchez and the man both looked at what was left of the bridge. It was hard to be what it once was. There was still smoke coming out of the wreckage. The result of the 5-inch gun. No doubt. The man explained that the cargo on the deck was brought on in Muscat. The crew that came with the crates also got on in Muscat. These men were obviously not experienced deckhands and rarely talked or even ate with the regular crew. They would get their food and then go back to sitting around the crates. The captain told them that this cargo was being transported for a friend of the owner. They did not know his name.

The XO inspected the numerous crates on the deck. Many had small arms, rifles, pistols, and grenades in them. Some still had RPGs. The ones fired at the ship and the helicopter were just a small fraction of the ones still in the crates. There were three larger crates on the deck. The XO got a crowbar and opened one of them. Inside, there appeared to be some type of heavy machine gun. It was huge. It had to be 5 feet long. Sanchez grabbed it with one hand and tried to move it. He could not. This thing was heavy.

"Anyone know what this is?" Sanchez yelled.

Boatswain's Mate First Class Lincoln approached. He looked at it for a moment and said, "It looks like a Russian DShK machine gun. Like our 50 caliber weapon. Good against people, vehicles, or aircraft. Not much good against a tank. This one looks a bit different. It might be a Type 54 or an MGD-12.7. I am not sure."

Sanchez was amazed. "How do you know all this, and what the heck is a Type 54 or the other thing?" Lincoln smiled, "I like to know about weapons that might be used against me. If they had fired this at the deck crew, we would have a lot more dead and a lot less wounded. The Type 54 is a Chinese rip-off of the DShK, and the MGD is an Iranian variation.

Sanchez was impressed. "Sure glad they didn't use these against us.

Sanchez, aided by his sailors and a few remaining crew members of the Whale, spent a few hours putting out the fires and getting the Whale underway. Lawrence once again told himself how lucky he was to have such a qualified XO. When all this was over, he would write Sanchez up for an award. Lawrence contacted Captain Stanford. He explained what was found on the Whale and that the Casey should escort it to a friendly port. A detailed inspection should be conducted, and the parent company of the ship should be notified.

"We will need some folks to debrief the crew in their own language and others to evaluate the cargo," said Lawrence. Captain Stanford agreed and directed Casey to escort the Whale to King Fahd Industrial Port in Saudi Arabia. There, both civilian and Navy intelligence personnel would debrief the crew of the Casey and the Whale.

The XO and his team would stay on the Whale until it was docked in Saudi Arabia. The Casey would closely escort the cargo ship.

No telling what other surprises might show up. One thing troubled him: how was he going to get Lieutenant Hawkins and the Seahawk back on board? Even with full fuel tanks, it would be a long flight to rejoin the Casey. He'd better get hold of Captain Stanford and let him work it out. He knew he would be writing reports and answering questions for several days.

Chapter Seven

It had been a beautiful morning. The sky was clear, and the seas were calm. Who could have guessed that the world would be turned upside down and the largest manhunt in the history of the United States would have been initiated today? Mohammad was in his home when the telephone rang. He had just finished breakfast and was getting ready to go to the office. There were many matters that needed his attention today.

The call was from an acquaintance from the King Fahd Industrial Port in Saudi Arabia. This was one of the stops made on occasion by the family's shipping line. They were always polite and professional.

"Good morning, how are you today?" asked Mohammad.

"I have some terrible news for you," came the reply. "The American Navy just brought in The Whale to the port. It is severely damaged, and there are many dead on board."

Mohammad was shocked. The Whale was an unarmed cargo ship. It flew the Iranian flag. It was not carrying cargo. What could have happened?

"Is my father safe?" he asked.

"I am trying to find out. The ship's bridge is destroyed, and there is severe damage to the superstructure, but she seems intact."

Mohammed screamed, "I do not care about the ship. How is my father?"

"I have a contact at the pier. I will call you back as soon as I find out."

The next hours were the longest in his life. Mohammed paced around the house. He could not understand what happened. Maybe pirates attacked the Whale and the Americans drove them off and escorted the ship to a safe port? No, his father would have called him. Maybe his father was injured and was being treated. That made more sense. He kept looking at the telephone, willing it to ring. It did not. No matter what happened, he would have to go there. His father might need help. Getting a complete crew and repairs would certainly take some effort. He could be packed in 30 minutes. He would charter a private aircraft to take him there. He would not want to sit near to some tourist on the flight. A commercial flight would take at least nine hours with one stop. Most flights took much longer with several stops. He started packing. Then the phone rang.

"I have some very bad news," his contact said. "I talked to one of the crew. I did not trust the Americans to give me the entire story. The Whale stopped in Muscat. Your father met Ahmed."

"I know him, he is a snake, but my father's friend," replied Mohammed.

"Ahmed asked your father to transport some crates and provided a deck crew to load and, apparently, guard the crates. The Americans must have found out and tried to stop the ship. The deck crew opened fire on an American warship, and the Americans returned fire and severely damaged the Whale. They brought the ship to port here. There is no trace of your father."

"What do you mean?" screamed Mohammed.

"Your father was on the bridge with the ship's captain when the American warship fired its main gun into the bridge. There are no remains." Mohammed was stunned beyond words. He could not talk; he could not move. He stared out the window, and the rage grew inside him.

Mohammad called the office. "Charter a jet, now. I have to go to Yanbu immediately."

"You have several meetings today, and that would be extremely expensive." Came his executive assistant's voice over the phone.

Mohammad bellowed, "I do not care about expense. I want a jet, and I want it now. Have a car waiting for me when I land, and book me a room at a hotel. Before you ask, I do not know how long I will be away. The Whale has been attacked, and my father may be dead." There was silent on the line.

"I will have it done immediately." Came the response.

Mohammad drove himself to the airport. He was speeding, of course. He didn't care. He drove up to the private terminal and saw the Bombardier 7500 waiting for him. He left his car and ran to the stairway. He carried his one bag on board and told the pilot to take off. He refused tea. Someone would park his car for him. He wanted to be on the other side of the Arabian Peninsula right now. Even this jet could not do that. As fast as a commercial airliner, it would still take hours to get to Yanbu. Any other time, he would have enjoyed the comfort and the privacy. Now his mind raced with so many questions. After about 3 hours of flight, a crew member came back and handed him a piece of paper. It was from his executive assistant back in Bandar Abbas. A Jaguar sedan would be waiting for him at the airport, and he was checked into the Holiday Inn in Yanbu. He had heard it was an excellent hotel, but right now that did not matter to him.

Several hours later, the sleek jet landed. He thanked the pilot as he exited the door and went down the ladder. He saw the silver Jaguar waiting for him. His assistant had "arranged" for him to bypass customs. He had nothing illegal with him, but he did not want to waste time with an inspection. He rocketed south towards the center of town. He had no time for sightseeing. He turned southeast onto Highway 5. After a few minutes, it turned into Route 55. He turned right onto Al-Mina. Minutes later, he turned left onto King Fahad Road. Within minutes, he was pulling up to the Sea Port Terminal. He parked the

Jaguar and looked around. He did not see The Whale. He walked into the terminal and asked for directions to where his ship was.

He introduced himself to the man seated at a desk in the lobby. The man had never seen Mohammad before but knew his name. The shipping company that he and his father ran was one of the largest in the area. The port did business with them on a regular basis. The man expressed his sadness over the loss of Bijan. He was a kind and fair man. He treated his workers well. He told Mohammad that his ship and the Navy ship were berthed at the piers on the other side of the waterway. Mohammad thanked the man and returned to his Jaguar. He drove north for about a quarter of a mile and then turned right. When he got to the oil treatment facility, he turned right again. A few moments later, he made the final right turn. This road would take him directly onto the pier where the Whale was. As he went down the road, he could see the Whale in the distance. At first, she looked fine. As he got closer, he could see the severe damage to the superstructure; the bridge was missing. His hands tightened on the steering wheel. He thought he might break it, but he didn't care. As he drew closer, he could see some kind of warship parked at the next pier. It flew the American Flag and had some damage visible. He didn't care. He stopped the Jaguar near the gangplank of the Whale. It was being guarded by several armed people in uniform. As he approached, he could see the writing on their chest, "U.S. Marines." Why was the American military guarding his ship? He approached them and identified himself as the owner of the shipping line and of that ship and demanded to be let aboard so he could inspect his ship.

The Marine said, "Sorry, Sir, my orders are not to allow any unauthorized personnel on board."

"Unauthorized?" he yelled. This is my ship, my family owns it."

The Marine thought and said, "Let me get you an officer to explain and see if he will let you aboard." The Marine said something into a microphone clipped to his collar. Mohammed fumed. He needed an American's permission to go onto his own ship.

"Sir, someone will be here in a moment to help."

A few minutes later, a car pulled up. Two men exited the car and walked towards Mohammed. One was in some kind of camouflaged uniform, the other wore slacks and a dress shirt. Mohammed did not wait for introductions. He walked to the men and told them who he was and that he was the owner of this ship. He demanded to know what had happened and where his father was. Where was his crew? The man in the uniform identified himself as Commander Stephen Turner, United States Navy. The other man did not identify himself.

Turner said, "I know you have a lot of questions, and I will try to answer them for you. First, let me express my deepest regrets on the loss of your father, the ship's captain, and several crew members."

There are two injured crew members at Yanbu General Hospital. They have minor injuries and should be released within a day or so. I have a list of the dead. They were identified by other members of your crew. The commander opened a folder and handed Mohammed a typed list of names.

"We did not find remains of your father and the ship's captain. They were on the bridge when fighting started. We also cannot identify the dead who were not part of your ship's crew and got on in Muscat."

"Who got on in Muscat? This was to be known as how do you say, a "shakedown" voyage." Turner shook his head. "I will tell you what I know. Most of the information came from your crewmembers." Turner told Mohammed that the ship had docked in Muscat. "Your father was seen on the dock with a man whom they identified as someone called 'Ahmed'. Mohammed stiffened; he knew Ahmed and some of his less-than-honest dealings. "Your father directed the crew to load several large crates on the deck. This Ahmed provided about a dozen men to go with the crates. These men, according to your crew, seemed to be guarding the crates, even while at sea." Mohammad did not like where this was going. "Everything was fine until the Whale came across a US Navy destroyer," continued Turner. "The destroyer had received information that the Whale was carrying contraband. The destroyer signaled the Whale to slow down to be inspected. The ship used flashing lights and voice communication in both English and Farsi. The Whale accelerated. The Whale was also being followed by a

U.S. Navy helicopter. The crew that came on board in Muscat opened some of the crates and removed numerous weapons. A rocket-propelled grenade was fired at the helicopter. The shot missed, and the helicopter did not return fire." Mohammed sighed. At least someone used restraint. "As the two ships passed each other," Stanford continued, "The men on the deck of the Whale opened fire with automatic weapons and the RPGs. Several American sailors were killed, and many more were wounded. The bridge took extensive damage. The destroyer returned fire until the firing stopped. Your ship was boarded. The wounded were treated as well as possible."

"I do not believe my father or his crew would do such a thing. We are into commercial shipping, not terrorism, as you Americans think all Iranians are." Mohammed said, looking directly into the eyes of the Naval Officer.

"As best we can tell," said Stanford, "none of the regular crew fired a single round. That your father had nothing to do with the attack. This is information gathered from the crew of the Whale. One of your crewmen said he believes he saw one of the "deck crew" holding your father and the captain at gunpoint." This made more sense to Mohammed; his father was a good man.

"Then explain to me why my father is dead." "The captain of the American ship had no way to know who was in charge of the attack. The men on the Whale fired first, killing members of his crew."

"Why did they have to use such powerful weapons on the Whale?" asked Mohammed.

"Numerous rocket-propelled grenades had already been fired, and the US crew could see more being readied. The captain, like any captain, has a duty to protect his crew and ship." Stanford hoped this answer was good enough.

"When can I inspect my ship? Your Marines will not let me on my own ship," asked Mohammed

"We have an inspection team on your ship now. All damage is being photographed, all military weapons are being inventoried, and then will be removed. We are also searching for anyone on the ship. They may be injured or hiding. Once this is done and our investigation is complete, we will return your ship to you. The crew members have already been interviewed and are free to leave."

Mohammed needed to talk to the crew, his crew, and get the story from them. The American sounded sincere, but he did not fully trust Americans. Once he got the whole story, he would. What would he do? What could he do? He had to think.

He got back into the Jaguar and drove to the hospital. Once inside, he explained who he was and that he wanted to see his employees. He would also cover any hospital expenses. He found them all in the same room. It was large but a bit too Spartan for his taste. The men were in good spirits. The nurse said they could be released within a day or so. They would be fine. He was grateful for that. These men had served his father and himself for many years. After the nurse left the room, Mohammed spoke to each of them to find out what really happened. He was surprised to learn that the American officer had spoken the truth. That Ahmed's men started shooting first. With most, if not all of Ahmed's men either dead or wounded, Mohammed could not understand the need for the bridge and superstructure to be destroyed. Surely, the Americans could have waited a little longer for the shooting to stop. His father was dead. Dead by American guns. This could not be tolerated. Someone would have to pay for this. Ahmed would have to pay, too. These actions could not be overlooked. Mohammad thanked them, wished them well, and told them that when they are ready, he would have a plane take them home. A paid vacation to follow. On the way out of the hospital, he talked to the nurse. He assured her that his company would pay for treatment and wanted the best for his men while they were there. The nurse thanked him and assured him of first-class treatment. Mohammed exited the hospital, got in the Jaguar, and headed for his hotel. He had many things to think about.

Mohammed got to his hotel. He did not even remember driving there. His only thoughts were about his father. The ship could be repaired. His men would heal. Once the shooting had started, they ran for cover. Ahmed's men stood up and opened fire. How stupid. He did not care that they had died. He walked past the large swimming pool. A few people were splashing around, having a good time. He wanted none of that. He entered his room. He was not hungry, he was not thirsty, he just burned inside. His father was dead because of Ahmed and the Americans. They both would pay and pay dearly. But how? He sat on the edge of the bed and stared into the mirror. He just sat there and stared. Hours went by. It became dark outside. He just sat there. Rage building. Then he realized what needed to be done. Ahmed must die. There could be no doubt of that. He didn't care how; he just wanted him dead. The Americans, on the other hand, had to be different. He could not kill them all. He could not attack the vessel that killed his father. In the year 2000, an American ship, similar to the one that killed his father, was attacked in Yemen. Seventeen sailors were killed, and several dozen were wounded. The ship did not sink. In fact, the Americans rebuilt it to show resolve. Since then, security for Navy ships had greatly increased. He doubted he could do it again with the results he wanted. He had to do something of such a nature that the Americans would stay home and be scared. Something that caused people throughout the country to scream and cry. Some that affected not just one city or building. Something that would paralyze them with fear for years to come. But what?

Chapter Eight

Several days later, Mohammed went home. He had arranged for his men to fly home. He had arranged to have the Whale brought back to Bandar Abbas. The ship's superstructure and the bridge were severely damaged and would probably have to be replaced. If the Americans could rebuild their ship, then he could also. The ship traveled slowly, but it would make it home.

Once home, several local government and religious leaders came to his home. They all expressed their sorrow and regret. Everyone was very polite. It was meaningless. Mohammed wanted to do something, had to do something. He was not sure what. The frustration level deep inside him was boiling over.

One of the local religious leaders, Masoud Hejazi, approached him. "Can we speak in private. Please" Mohammed showed him into his home office and closed the door. "First, let me say how sorry we all are. Your father was a very good man and a great asset to the community and the country. We will all miss him. He was a fair and honest businessman."

"Thank you." Said Mohammed.

"How are you handling this?" the cleric asked.

"I am so frustrated, a friend of my father betrayed him and caused his death. The American Navy overreacted. They could have handled this so much better. I need to do something."

"What is it you want to do?" asked the cleric. Mohammad thought, then the emotions boiled over.

"I want Ahmed dead; I want America to pay. Pay as they never had before. Something worse than the Twin Towers,"

The cleric told him, "I have a friend. I will have him stop by. He can help you."

"How?" asked Mohammad.

"I will let him explain that to you himself."

The rest of the day had friends and relatives coming and going. He wished they would all just leave. He had to think. He had to find a way to vent his rage. Having Ahmed killed would not be hard. Destroying America would be much more difficult. No conventional attack could succeed. Hijacking was not reliable due to all the security measures the Americans put on their airlines. No, not by air. He was a sailor at heart and now had control of a major shipping company. How could that be used? He could have a ship full of explosives blow up a dock or harbor. That would only affect a few coastal cities. Prices would rise due to the lack of shipments, but the American would just go on. "It happened somewhere else," they would think. No, that would not be enough. Maybe this friend of Masoud Hejazi would have some thoughts.

Brian Maxwell was sitting at his desk when the phone rang. "This is Navy Captain Stanford calling from CENTCOM. Please go secure." Classified material should never be discussed on an unsecure phone line. There were stickers on the phone reminding people of this. Phone calls are easily intercepted, and anything said would probably wind up in enemy hands or in a report on some counterintelligence security officer's desk. It could ruin a career. However, by pushing a button or two on a specially made phone, the conversation would be encrypted. Anyone listening in would hear something that would sound like the person was talking underwater. It would make no sense, and even if recorded, the conversation would be totally intelligible.

Maxwell "went secure." "What can I do for you, Captain?"

Stanford told Maxwell that it was his intelligence report that started the events leading up to the "situation which developed" between the Casey and the Whale. "It seems this Ahmed was shipping weapons to who knows where; his men panicked when they saw the Casey. They fired an RPG at the Seahawk and several at the Casey. There was a brief but intense exchange of gunfire. The Whale lost." Maxwell thought for a moment. It looked like his guess about the shipment was right.

"What can I do for you?"

Stanford replied, "I need everything you have on Ahmed and his activities. All his men are dead, and we will need to question him directly." "I doubt he will talk to you," said Maxwell.

"We are not going to give him that option," said Stanford. "Just send me everything you've got as soon as possible. This is time sensitive. Someone will decide who is going to visit him." Maxwell said he would send all files today.

Captain Stanford walked from his office and walked up to Lieutenant Commander Rodricks. Rodricks was the Navy Special Warfare Liaison to CENTCOM. "Rodricks, I think I have a job for your folks. Tell me what you think." There will be more information coming in today, but the short version is that this guy in Muscat loaded up a cargo ship with weapons, and his men used those weapons to engage the Casey. I am sure there are folks who want to talk to him. Can you see if your folks can do this, or should I get someone else?" Rodricks had heard about the Casey and the gun battle. It was almost enough to make him want to become a surface warfare officer, almost.

"Sure thing, skipper, just invite him to come back here and have a long talk?"

"That would be fine," said Stanford. "I do not expect him to be too heavily guarded, but the Agency will be sending over their file on him."

Rodricks rolled his eyes, "Then I am sure everything will be accurate and correct." Rodricks had had prior dealings with the C.I.A. and was not overly impressed. "This will be kind of short-fused. He must know about the shoot-out, and he may go to ground. Don't know, but would sure like to know where the weapons came from and where they are going," said Stanford. "I'll get on it right away. When the rest of the intel comes in, please make sure I get it anytime, day or night."

"No problem," Stanford replied.

At about the same time, a tall, thin man rang the doorbell at Mohammed's home. Mohammed answered the door and saw the man. He was wearing a black suit, a white shirt, and a black tie. He looked like some kind of business executive. The man spoke in a quiet voice.

"Masoud Hejazi said I might be able to help you."

Mohammed let him in. They walked to the living room. The man sat without an invitation to do so.

"Would you like some tea?" Mohammed asked.

"No, thank you," was the curt reply.

Mohammed did not like this man and was a bit scared of him. It was nothing he said or did, just a feeling, he thought.

"How can I help you?"

Mohammed thought and then made up his mind. "I want someone in Muscat dead. This man is the reason my father is dead."

"Is he Iranian? Asked the man.

"No, he is from Oman."

"Very well," came the answer. "Is there anything else I can help you with?"

Mohammed was shocked; just like that, he had asked and was granted the death of Ahmed. He felt strange, empowered, as if this were a minor business deal. "What will that cost me?" he asked.

"Nothing," came the answer. "Is there anything else you need?"

Mohammed was afraid to tell the man what he wanted. It was a bizarre scheme. It would cost the lives of many people and change how Americans lived and functioned. Could he trust this man?

"How do I know I can trust you? You could be someone from the security forces."

"I am," he said. "You have suffered a great wrong, which must be avenged. Masoud Hejazi said you were a good man and a dedicated Iranian. If your plan is sound, I will provide you with the items you need."

Mohammed thought about it for several minutes. He knew he could not succeed without help. He decided to trust this man. Mohammed explained he wanted to hurt all of America, all at the same time, in a manner that they could never recover from. A way to show the weakness of their government to protect them, a way to keep their military at home and not in the Middle East. The man said to continue, he was interested. Mohammed laid out his plan in detail. The man sat back and liked this plan. No one would see it coming, and even if they did, they could not stop it.

He thought for a few moments. "I will provide you with the equipment and men you need. Can you provide the transportation?"

"That will not be a problem, I have considerable resources," said Mohammed. "How long will it take you to find these men and have my supplies delivered?"

The man smiled, "Ahmed will be handled this week, as will be the supplies. The men will take at least 1 to 2 weeks, no more."

Mohammed was impressed. He was asking a lot. Fifty suicide bombers in less than 2 weeks. This man must have some very good connections. "I will arrange for their transportation. I have an acquaintance in Mexico; he can be trusted for enough money. We will use his home as a base of operations. The men will arrive over several weeks, so they will not know more than a few others.

Security will be kept very tight. Are you sure these men will do what is asked of them?"

The man looked at him, "They will do whatever you ask. The idea of destroying American is all the motivation they will need. Here is a card with a telephone number on it where you can always reach me." Mohammed looked at the card. "It does not have your name or address on it." "That is correct." The man smiled and let himself out of the home.

Chapter Nine

U.S. Navy Senior Chief Robert Evans looked at this team. The junior man had over five years' experience in Special Operations. Some had over twenty years. He had a good team. All had graduated from the BUD/S course. BUD/S was the Basic Underwater Demolition/SEAL course. Six months of the arguably toughest course in the United States military. Of course, they had to attend the basic airborne course. This allowed them to parachute with a static line into an operational area. However, that was not enough. Most had attended the MFF or Military Free Fall course. Civilians would think of this as skydiving. Civilians do not jump at night, over enemy territory with a hundred pounds of gear from five miles up without lights. After all that, a man still had to prove himself to his team. This could easily take 6 more months, depending on the operations encountered.

CENTCOM had ordered them on a mission with little notice and time to prepare. SEALS plan their operations in infinite detail. All options and possible problems needed to be addressed. Usually, a mockup of the target would be made and the operation rehearsed. They did not have that ability on this mission. The CENTCOM briefer told them it was a "simple" snatch and grab. Basically, a kidnapping on foreign soil. The target had information about terrorist arms shipments, contacts, and supply routes. The intelligence boys wanted a long talk with him. Their target was a businessman in Muscat. He was not known to be armed and might have had only one or two guards at his home. What could go wrong?

They would deploy from the deck of an LHA, an Amphibious Assault Ship. This ship was almost three football fields long. While it would look like an aircraft carrier to many, it was not. It did not have a catapult to launch aircraft, nor did it have the tradition four arresting cables to help stop a landing aircraft. Instead, it served a variety of helicopters, the V-22 Osprey, and the F-35B, stealth strike fighter. The last two aircraft could take off and land vertically on the deck.

At 0200 hours, Senior Chief Evans and his team boarded an Osprey. Besides their SCUBA gear, a variety of weapons, numerous tools, and a radio, the team loaded a Zodiac boat. They would fly from the Gulf of Oman to a point about two kilometers off the coast of Muscat. Once there, the Osprey would tilt its engines to the vertical and slow almost to a standstill. It would be almost motionless, for a few seconds, about 15 feet above the water. Evans and his men would push the Zodiac boat out the rear ramp of the aircraft. They would follow the boat by jumping from the aircraft with their gear. Special Warfare Operator First Class Washington would stay with the boat. The rest of the team would swim, underwater and without lights, to the shore and conduct the mission. Once the target was secured, Washington would bring the boat to the shore, where the team and the target would get on the boat and head for the open sea. They would be picked up by a Navy ship, which would be waiting for them. At least that is how the plan was supposed to go. Unknown to Evans and his team, other forces were at play.

At about the same time, Evans and his team were swimming towards Muscat Beach, a man in dark clothing was walking slowly on 37th Street in Muscat. He was near Athalba Beach. There was no one on the street. The man smiled, just as he had hoped. He approached a compound between 37 Street and the water. This would be Ahmed's home, Ahmed, his target. The man approached the wall around the house, and with what appeared to be little effort, jumped up and grabbed the top of the wall. He pulled himself over the top without making a sound. He quietly dropped down onto the soft soil and headed for the house.

At this time, Evans and his team had made it to the beach and were coming on shore. Their non-reflective suits kept them dry and stealthy. They moved like shadows through the streets, soundless. Aerial photography provided them with a detailed image of the area. They would be approaching the target's home in a few minutes. "Simple snatch and grab," they were told.

The man took a small 9mm pistol from inside his jacket. The only thing odd about it was that the barrel extended out past the front of the pistol. If anyone could see it clearly, they would have seen the threading on the outside of the extended barrel. Unlike television, the suppressor he attached had to screw on to something. It did not just clip onto the normal barrel. He waited a minute, standing perfectly still.

He saw both guards. One was standing by a tree in the shadows. The other, the stupid one, was smoking a cigarette. The glow made him plainly visible. This will be too easy. He walked so slowly to the man standing by the tree. At about seven feet, he fired. The 147-grain subsonic hollow point made almost no sound at all leaving the barrel. That it was subsonic, moving slower than the speed of sound, it did not make a sonic boom as it flew the short distance. It hit the guard in the side of his head. His brain destroyed, he dropped like a stone. The other guard heard nothing, or if he did, he did not react. The man took a two hand stance and fired twice. The first bullet hit the guard in the chest, punching a hole in his lung. He tried to process what had just happened when the second bullet impacted his neck. As the bullet expanded, it shredded his carotid artery. His brain deprived of blood, he dropped silently to the ground. The man now walked slowly to the rear of the house.

Senior Chief Evans could see the house. He was less than a half a block away. There was no street traffic. That was great. Evens did not want to shoot it out with a bunch of civilians. Just get in and get out. They careful walked up the driveway to the house. Their night vision goggles showed no one on guard. The intelligence report said two to four guards at any one time. The team advanced to the front door. There was a light on in the house. No noise could be heard. The team split in half. Each half positioned itself on either side of the door. Normally, entry would be made with plastic explosives to remove the door or a quick shotgun blast to each of the door hinges or the lock itself. This was to be a quiet extraction, so Evens had one of the team quietly work the lock with a set of picks. It should not take long.

The man in black was now inside the house. He moved slowly, quietly. He observed the furniture so that he would not run into anything. He slowly climbed the stairs to the bedroom. He looked around the house and realized that gun running must pay well. This was a very nice house. He got to the top of the stairs. The master bedroom was to the left. The bedroom door was open. He walked in. He made no sound. He could see Ahmed sleeping soundly. As he raised the pistol, he heard a click. It was faint, hardly noticeable. He did not survive this long, in this line of work, by not paying attention to the smallest detail. The sound came from downstairs. It would not be the security people. He had made sure of that. Someone was entering the house. Not friends, not family, and not more security. He had done his homework for this target. Who else could it be? Whoever it was, he did not want to meet them. He fired two shots at the sleeping figure. One struck Ahmed between the shoulder blades, striking his spine. The shot struck at the base of the skull where the spine connects. Either shot would have been fatal. The man did not take chances. He did not rise to the height of his profession by being careless. He heard the front door make the slightest of sounds as it opened. The man exited the bedroom window and dropped silently into the backyard.

He walked quickly to the wall and jumped over it. His mission was accomplished. He vanished into the night.

Evans and his men entered the house. As they had practiced so many times before, they slowly cleared every room, every closet, every hiding space to make sure they would not be surprised. They were still expecting to run into security personnel. Evans was concerned that no one was moving about the house. After the ground floor was secured, Evans took some of the men to clear the upstairs portion of the home. It was a very large home. He sent the rest of the team to clear the backyard and the garage. No sense taking chances. As they got to the second floor, Evans could smell it. You did not spend as much time as he did in special operations, and did not know the smell left by a weapon being fired. The smell was faint, but in such a clean home, it was obvious. Evans entered the master bedroom and saw Ahmed in bed. The bullet holes and blood were obvious. "We may have a shooter on the grounds, heads up," said Evans into his microphone to alert the team. Evans walked up to the body. He carefully checked Ahmed's wrist for a pulse. He also checked his throat. He knew the mission was a failure. That much blood in the head area was not a wound anyone could walk away from. He had to check; it would be a requirement for the debriefing. Evans ordered the team to assemble and leave the property. He did not want to explain why a group of armed Navy SEALS was in a dead man's bedroom.

The team exited the property and headed for the water. Evans sent a signal to Washington to come get them. It was going to be a long night.

Chapter Ten

The man in black returned to Bandar Abbas, his mission completed. Mohammed would be happy and grateful. The individual he hated the most was dead. No doubt the Americans would have wanted to speak to Ahmed. That would have been very awkward. He would have given up important information about gun smuggling. That would not be acceptable. As the saying goes, "Two birds with one stone."

The man in black went to Mohammed's home late in the evening. He did not need to be seen by anyone. Mohammed opened the door and let the man in. "I have good news for you. The assignment in Muscat has been completed."

"Are you sure?" Mohammad asked.

"Absolutely" was the response.

Mohammad sat down on the couch and smiled. Mohammed's mood changed. He looked at the man. "You never told me who you are. I know we have a mutual friend, but who are you really?"

"That is not important. We have similar goals. I am in a position to help you. Do you still wish to continue with your mission against the United States?" Mohammed thought and said that he did, more than ever.

"I have worked out more details. I now know where and when the attacks will be. I will pay for this out of my own funds. Can you provide the 'volunteers' and explosives?"

"That will not be a problem," said the man. "I will need everything by early May. Can you do this?" The man smiled. He knew this plan would work.

It would be easy to find fifty martyrs. Finding the explosives would be even easier. Mohammad did not want anything fancy or powerful. Just fifty reliable hand grenades, an easy task. The plan was so simple and so devastating, he wondered how Mohammad thought it up, and he didn't. It would send a shock wave across American. Every American would be affected. Everyone would know that their sense of safety was a lie. Americans would lose confidence in their leaders, their military, and their law enforcement. The news media would have dozens of stories to tell, film footage from all over the country. Americans would be bombarded with news media showing the carnage from all over the country around the clock for many days. The American news media would help to assure mission success. Yes, this would be a great mission.

Chief Evans sat before a review panel. While it is common to have a "hot wash," a review, after each mission, he had never seen so much brass in attendance. There were also several "suits" in the room. No one looked happy. "OK, Senior Chief. Let's go over it again." This was the fourth time he gave the group a detailed account of what happened. No, he had not seen or heard the shooter. No, none of his men could have leaked the information about the mission. No, no one was alerted by their presence in Muscat. The mission was textbook, except for the results. Evans looked to Commander Morgan, the senior SEAL in the room, for help. Morgan shook his head and then let it drop to his chest. Morgan knew that Evans and his team did everything right. The CIA knew that they had done something wrong; otherwise, Ahmed would be in their custody and answering questions. The Navy must have done something wrong. How else to account for the failure? Evans did not know the answer. He never would know, and neither would the others in the room.

Chapter Eleven

It was the first week of May, and Mohammed was getting nervous. He had not heard from the man in several weeks. The clock was ticking, and Mohammed had eight weeks to go. Then the world would know Iran's power and reach. The world would know the American failure. But only if this agent or spy or whatever he is came through. The last few weeks had been stressful. There were separate funerals for his father and the ship's captain. He personally checked on every member of the ship's crew. He made sure they had healed and could return to work. That was after a two-week vacation for each crew member and their families. Mohammed may want to be a mass murderer, but he took care of his people.

On May 7th, the man appeared at Mohamed's home at 9:00 PM. Mohammed was finishing up some paperwork at home when the doorbell rang. The same man, in the same suit, with the same expression on his face. Mohammed wondered if this man had any other clothes to wear.

"I had not heard from you in a while and thought maybe you had changed your mind about supposing me," said Mohammed.

"No, the plan is still going to happen. I have your explosives and your fifty volunteers. Each man knows this is a suicide mission. They also know that they will cause more damage to America than anyone else could do, without using nuclear weapons. They know their names will be engraved on a monument for their actions. Their families will have hero status in our country. They will all die for you, without hesitation."

"When can you bring them to me?" Mohammed asked. They will not be fully briefed until we are all in Mexico. No person, other than myself, will know the entire plan. Security must be maintained at all costs. Anyone who interferes with the mission will be dealt with immediately."

The man raised his hand, "Do not worry. They know what is expected of them. I can have everything here in two days."

"Very well," said Mohammed. "We will leave on the night of the 9th. Can you bring them and the explosives to my company dock by 8 PM?" "My company dock," thought Mohammed, it sounded so strange. It had always been his father's dock or the family dock. Now it was his dock.

"We will have them all on board, and we will get underway immediately. I am sure there are eyes watching my dock, besides yours." The man smiled. It was the biggest smile he had seen on the man's face.

Mohammed had a lot to do in the next two days. He would be coming back from this mission, so the business had to be run normally to prevent suspicion. His friend and deputy director would run the company in his absence. If anyone asked, he would be taking a needed vacation after the death of his father. He wanted a change of scenery. He would be vacationing in Central America. He would be exploring and maybe do some camping on his own. He needed a rest. This would explain why his ship would be traveling to Mexico. He would have to arrange transposition for all these men. Customs would not be a problem. It is amazing what can be accomplished with money. A month's salary to take an early lunch would be a strong motivator.

On the evening of the 9th, two busloads of men drove up to the dock. Each man carried just one piece of luggage. That would make them look more like tourists. Each man got off the bus and walked up the gangway and onto the ship. No one said a word. The last four men were singled out. There were two wooden crates in the back of one of the buses. Each crate was carried by two men holding the rope handles on the side of the crate. The crates were heavy but not so much that the four men could not carry the two crates. Once on the ship, one of the ship's crew directed them to an area where they could place the crates. Two other crew members directed the men into the ship's interior. There, they would be directed to their sleeping area. A large room with numerous beds and hammocks. This was not a luxury cruise. Each man knew he would be dead soon. No need to complain about the sleeping arrangement.

The ship sailed several hours later. There was nothing remarkable about the departure. A few words from Mohammad and a look from the man in black to the port authorities made sure things went smoothly. Somehow, the paperwork for the departing ship had disappeared. There would be no record of the departure. The ship stayed in the normal shipping lanes. Cruising at a normal speed so as not to attract attention. The trip would take several weeks. They had to be in Mexico by the end of the month. Until then, the men had little to do except dream of paradise. The food on the ship was surprisingly good. The only complaint was that only a few men at a time could go on deck at any one time. If a passing ship or aircraft saw #50 men on the deck, it might raise suspicion. Of course, there were those spy satellites to worry about.

The voyage went smoothly. The weather was good and the seas calm. The men on board took this to be an omen. They struck the Americans in their hearts and brought her to her knees. A wonderful way to die. The ship made several stops for fuel. The men stayed below decks. No one would know they were there. Crossing the Atlantic was a bit rougher. The sea was choppy, and it was windy. Several of the men got seasick. The others made fun of them. The ship continued westward.

After weeks of travel, the ship made land. They would dock in the city of Tampico. None of the men had ever been there before. They were not there for tourism. Each man picked up his one bag and walked down the gangway. It was good to be on land again. The weather was warm and sunny. As they set foot on the dock, they were directed to two buses. As they got on the bus, a short, elderly man handed them a brown paper bag. Their luggage was stowed in an area on the side of the bus. Almost every man opened the bag to see what the content was. The bag contained fresh fruit, sandwiches, and two bottles of water. There would be no rest stops for these buses. Each had a restroom. The buses would drive to a home in Mexico. They were told this would be their base until they left for the United States. They were not given any more information. They were told not to get friendly with the person seated next to them. This was for security purposes. The men were happy to be on land. After eating, most slept or thought about what they were going to do. The buses drove on. They stopped several times for fuel. The men were not allowed to leave the bus. At each stop, the driver would go into the cargo area of the bus and get another bag of food for the men. There would be no going to a truck stop for a hot meal. No one would see any of them. They would eat, sleep, and use the bus restroom. It was as if they were never there.

After a full day of driving, the bus had reached its destination. The buses pulled into the large driveway of the home. The men were told to get off the bus and take their garbage with them. Once outside, they got their luggage from under the bus. As soon as this was done, the buses left. They stood around and looked at the huge home.

As they stood around, not knowing what to do next, Mohammed walked out of the front door and approached them.

"I am the person who will lead you on your mission to kill Americans. I will provide you with all instructions and equipment. Until you leave this house, I am your leader and master. Any violation of the rules will result in two things. First, your immediate death. No excuses or reasons, I will shoot you myself. If you force me to kill you, you will let down your brothers and sisters, you will let down your country, and you will let down your heritage. These are unpardonable sins. While here, you will eat well and rest. You will receive any training you may need. You will be issued your equipment."

He let that sink in. "There are a few basic security rules. No one will leave this compound under penalty of death. The next time you leave, it will be for the mission. You will not use names here. If you are caught and cannot kill yourself, you will not be able to give the names of your brothers, even under torture. You will not discuss your mission with your brothers. Not any part of it. Again, for security. In a few minutes, you will enter the home and be assigned a place to sleep. Meals will be served in shifts. These times will be posted. Once you enter this home, you will not say or use your name. You will be assigned a number. This is your new identity. Your assignment is based on this number. Before you leave here, you will be issued a fake passport, a driver's license, money, and other paperwork. Hopefully, none of you will be stopped by American authorities. If you do as you are told, you will succeed in your mission and the United States will collapse on itself." The men cheered and then started to walk to the house.

Once inside the huge house, Mohammed gave each man a card. The card had a number. No two people had the same number. This would be who they are until their death. The numbers ranged from 1 to 50. There was no apparent reason for the number they were given. No one asked about someone else's number. Mohammad's warning about instant death had a chilling effect. "There are bedrooms upstairs. After dinner, you will go to your room. Your number will be posted on the entrance to the room. Rest and read The Book. You will not be allowed to take it with you. After the morning meal, you will learn your purpose."

Chapter Twelve

The fifty men assembled in front of the house. They had slept well and eaten better. This Mohammed knows how to take care of his men. Mohammed stood before them. He stood slightly higher than the group, in the entrance way of the house. "We are here to destroy America," yelled Mohammad. The men roared their approval with both shouts and throat noises. "The Americans feel they can do what they want. That they are safe because their borders are protected by oceans and friendly countries. We stand in one right now. So much for safety." The men laughed. "The Americans were shocked when the Japanese blew up some military ships in 1941. The next time was when the Twin Towers and the Pentagon were attacked. Those actions made them mad. Those actions only hit a few of their states. We will not make them mad; we will make them terrified." Again, the men screamed their support of attacking the United States. "We will attack every state, at the same time, on their holiday, their Independence Day." The men screamed at the top of their lungs. They would not stop even when Mohammed waved at them to stop. They finally stopped and looked at Mohammad. They had never heard of him, and now he would lead them to glory, martyrdom, and the destruction of America.

"Each one of you has been assigned a number. There are fifty states, and you are fifty in number. You will receive your specific instructions in a few days. You will all go to your target city. On July

4th, you will go to your specific target and be carried into Allah's arms by the explosive you will be issued. I will arrange your travel. You will go and do your assignment. The Americans will be paralyzed with fear. You will set off an explosive in a populated part of each state's capital. Every American will be afraid. Afraid of you and afraid of us. They will not be able to send their military to our countries because they will be restoring order in their own country. Every American will be afraid. Every state will be struck. Are you with me?" The roar from the group was deafening. Mohammed knew this mission would succeed. Death to America.

For the next week, the men were given classes on how to act, what to say, and how not to attract attention. What to do if questioned by authorities. They were issued American-looking clothing. Mostly jeans and a dress shirt. No one would notice that. Running shoes were issued. No sandals allowed. It was stressed several times a day that no one should discuss their particular mission with anyone else. They guessed correctly that their number had something to do with which state they were going to.

Some were given haircuts and shaves. They protested that this violated their religious beliefs, but were assured they would be forgiven due to their martyrdom. They must not draw attention to themselves. There were still many Americans who would eye them suspiciously unless they blended in. They were taught how to pump and pay for gasoline. Many of them would drive to their target cities. Since most of them would only be in the United States for about a week, they could eat at fast-food drive-throughs or food bought at truck stops along their route. They could sleep at motels along the route to their target. Their false passport and driver's licenses should be good enough for identification. They would pay cash. Their story is that they were tourists and sightseeing in America. They must obey all traffic laws. Their fake driver's license would not stand up to detailed inspection by the police. Mohammed had no way to enter the information into each state's computer system.

They would leave staggered in the order of who had to go the furthest. Two of them would receive special instructions for their trip. Mohammed did not want 50 men crossing the border on one day. True, they would cross at different locations, but the Border Patrol computer system was linked to each other. This mission was too important to fail. America must pay.

Mohammad made the final travel preparations. Some would travel by car, others by bus or train. The first two to leave would go by land and sea. This could have been a little complicated. Decades of working in the shipping industry made these plans easy for him. He finally finished his plans. The buses would pick up the men, several each day, and take them to various border towns. They would be dropped off inside the United States. From there, they would rent cars, take buses, or trains. They would arrive a day or two before July 4th. Once in their target city, they would do a reconnaissance of the actual target. On the 4th, at the same time, they would detonate their explosives and cause fear and panic, the likes of which Americans had never known. His father would be avenged.

The day before the first group left, Mohammed would sit down with each man. He would explain their route and their mission. They would get to know where they were going and what their target was. They would not attack military bases. Most Americans do not serve in the armed forces. Americans would see an attack on a base as soldiers doing their job. Bases are also defended. A shoot-out at the front gate would not accomplish the mission. No, America must be hit where the everyday person would feel the effects of the attack. Civilian blood must be spilled.

Chapter Thirteen

The first to leave were numbers #49 and #50. They were taken by car to San Antonio, Texas. From there, they both boarded an Amtrak train to Los Angeles, California. The trip took almost 2 days. The men sat apart. They did not speak to each other or even make eye contact. Security was paramount. They both sat in a regular seat. They looked out the window or slept. There were several stops along the way. They used the money Mohammed gave them to buy food and drinks. They enjoyed the American food. They especially liked the chocolate. They could not enjoy this in their home country. Upon arriving in Los Angeles, they took separate cabs to the Port of Los Angeles. This port is over 400 acres of working people from numerous countries. The entire facility is about 7500 acres. This includes both land and water work areas. With millions of containers moving through the port annually, security is severely strained. Two additional people walking around barely raised an eyebrow.

Their orders had them report to different piers. Mohammad, with all his contacts in the shipping industry, found no problem getting them booked on two different ships. One was headed up the inland passage way to Alaska, and the other was going directly to Honolulu, Hawaii. Both trips would take the better part of a week. As the trip was within the United States, there was no customs inspection. Their fake IDs and being on the ship's manifest got them aboard without any problems. The ships sailed later that day. It would take many days to get to their destinations. Honolulu would be warm and sunny. Juneau would be rainy. It didn't matter; they would be dead soon. These capitols would know fear and panic.

While #49 and #50 were sailing to their destinations, more and more of the men departed the beautiful house in Mexico. Those going the furthest would go by train or bus. Those going within one or two days would go by car. Mohammed had to make sure those going by car could drive and do so safely. An accident would ruin the plans. Luckily, he had found several men who were excellent drivers. They would be the last to leave as they were going the shortest distance. They could leave on the 1st or 2nd of July. They would be in their target city and have a day to check out their targets. It would take little rehearsal. Find the target, walk up to a crowd of people, and at the exact time, detonate their explosives.

The buses took the men to several different locations. It might raise suspicion if dozens of men appeared at a car rental company or a train station. The two buses would load men in the morning and then leave. One bus would cross the border at Reynosa, and the other would cross at Laredo. The bus that crossed Reynosa would drive another 3 hours and drop the men off at Corpus Christi, Texas. From there, they could take a bus or train to the various capitols they planned to attack. The other bus, which crossed at Laredo, would take the men to San Antonio, Texas. Again, they could take a train or a bus to the various capitals around the lower 48 states. Mohammed worried about something going wrong. He had planned for all contingencies. However, he thought it wise to have a few men drive to their targets. They would be the last to leave. They would be useful in making sure nothing was left behind in the house as evidence of them even being there. Mohammed did not care about the owner of the house. He was a cartel member and would be paid handsomely for the use of the home. However, if authorities ever discovered the home, he wanted nothing there to link him to the mission. The cartel had provided three older model sedans. The last three men would drive to Austin, Texas, Oklahoma City, Oklahoma, and Baton Rouge, Louisiana. All three cities were within a day's drive. The drivers would take their time, obey all traffic laws, and get to their target city on the 2nd of July. This would allow for traffic problems and get there in time to walk around the target.

Prior to departure, each man was given two American-made M67 fragmentation grenades. Mohammed liked the idea of using American military equipment against Americans. After all, it was US equipment that killed his father. These grenades were light, less than a pound each, and would kill or wound anyone within 5 meters or about 16 ½ feet. Their instructions were to throw one grenade into a crowd of people and then run into another group, detonate the grenade, killing more people and themselves. His friend in black provided the grenades without a problem. Probably stolen from some American base in Iraq or Afghanistan. Mohammed didn't care, as long as they worked. Their target would be the largest shopping mall in the target city. The idea was not to kill as many people as possible, just to instill fear in all 50 states at the same time. 100 explosions on their holiday would do that. It would also keep people from shopping, thus damaging the economy. Mohammed had to make sure that each man knew what time to explode their devices. There were six time zones in play here.

Man #50 was due to detonate his devices at 3:00 P.M. in the Royal Hawaiian Center. It was located on Kalakaua Avenue. It would be a short cab ride from the harbor where the ship carrying him would dock. Man #49, who also traveled by ship, would attack the Mendenhall mall in Juneau, Alaska, at 4:00 P.M. Man #49 wanted to attack Anchorage, the largest city in the state. That would probably get him a higher body count. Mohammed refused to allow this; only capitols, seats of government, would be attacked. This was for psychological reasons. If you cannot protect your capitols, what can you protect?

Each man was given an envelope with the name and address of the shopping mall they were to attack. They were also told what time to attack. The 48 states had four different time zones. Timing was of paramount importance to create fear and panic. To overwhelm their phone lines. To sow chaos, their news media would help do that. Every elected official would want their own airtime on television. Social media would crash due to chat overloads and people up loading video rather than helping their neighbors. This would be a glorious day.

Chapter Fourteen

It was a warm summer day. Of course, every summer day in El Paso, Texas, is warm. Hector Ramirez was at work. To him, being a Texas State Trooper was not work. It is what he always wanted to be. As a child, he had seen troopers on the road. Their cars were always clean, and their uniforms were always professional. Clean and crisp. Born and raised in El Paso, Ramirez graduated from a local high school and got a Bachelor's degree in criminal justice from the University of Texas at El Paso. He was so proud of his UTEP school ring. He was the first person in his family to get a four-year degree. He applied to the Texas Department of Public Safety to become a State Trooper. He was accepted and sent to the DPS Academy. It was a long course, taking many months. Both academics and physical fitness were stressed. Being a live-in academy had its benefits and drawbacks. You could be worked day and night. Shooting and driving classes were held throughout the day and night. Not commuting home after work every day allowed him to study more. By the time he finished studying, it was time to sleep. The first few weeks seemed to have harassment. This was to weed out those who did not really want the job. Ramirez did not think it was that much of a bother. He graduated 2nd in his class. When asked what assignment he wanted, he asked to go back to El Paso. He knew the area, had friends and family there, and being fluent in Spanish would be a definite help.

So, on this bright sunny day, Texas State Trooper Ramirez, driving his black and white SUV, was patrolling Interstate Ten in El Paso County. Some of the new troopers had hoped for one of the high-speed Dodge pursuit vehicles. He was happy with his comfortable Ford SUV. It had more interior space in the vehicle for his gear. It was a much better vehicle to go off-road with.

He was getting ready for his lunch break. There were numerous fast-food businesses along the Interstate. He then made a mistake that every cop knows about. Never say, "One more stop." These always go bad. This one would save America. He saw a newer Corvette weaving through traffic. The car was about 15 miles per hour over the speed limit. It was also cutting in and out of traffic, without signaling. The car also cut off an SUV. Ramirez needed to talk to the driver.

He accelerated his police vehicle and got behind the Corvette. The car was 15 over the posted limit. Ramirez activated his emergency red and blue lights. One never knew what would happen next. Was it a kid, an elderly person, a criminal fleeing the scene of a crime? One never knows. Luckily, the car pulled over immediately. It even signaled that it was pulling over. Ramirez stopped about a car length behind the vehicle. As her exited his SUV, he made sure to check behind him. He did not want to lose his car door to a gust of wind from a passing 18-wheeler. He carefully approached the car, just like he was taught in the academy. One never knew who one was stopping. He made sure to stand at the end of the Corvette's door. This made the driver turn to look at the officer. Again, a safety measure.

The driver was a Hispanic man, only a few years older than Ramirez. He was wearing a nice suit, but without a tie. Ramirez looked at his hand. No weapons and nothing nearby. Again, that safety training.

"Good afternoon, sir. I am Trooper Ramirez, Texas Department of Public Safety. I stopped you for your speed and not signaling several lane changes. May I please see your license and proof of insurance?" The man smiled, not a care in the world, reached into his jacket pocket, got his license and insurance, and handed them to Ramirez. Ramirez took the paperwork. "Please wait in your vehicle. I will be back with you in a few minutes."

Ramirez walked back to his police vehicle. He had to look in two directions at once, at the driver of the vehicle and at oncoming traffic. Many officers are hurt or killed by someone sideswiping a stopped police vehicle. Ramirez typed the man's name and driver's license number, as well as the license plate number, into the computer, which sits between the two front seats. While waiting for a response on the records check, Ramirez reviewed the proof of insurance. It was current and covered the Corvette. He looked up at the computer screen. It showed the vehicle registration to be current. It showed no warrants for the driver. The next screen showed that the license number was not in the file. "Stupid mistake," he thought. "I must have entered it wrong." He then reentered the number on the driver's license, as well as entered the man's name and date of birth from the driver's license. He was writing the traffic ticket for speeding when the results came back on the screen. There was no license with that number. The name and date of birth check showed a valid license, but with a different number, and the picture did not match the driver of the Corvette. Troopers can see the face that is supposed to be on the license on their computer screen.

Bells went off in his head. Something is very wrong here. An expensive car and a phony driver's license? Something is wrong. Ramirez got on the radio and asked for another unit for backup. There were no troopers nearby, but there was a sheriff's deputy in the area. Ramirez kept his eyes on the driver and waited. Three minutes later, an SUV belonging to the El Paso County Sheriff's Office pulled in behind him. Ramariz explained what was going on to the deputy.

Ramirez walked up to the driver's side of the Corvette. The deputy walked up to the car on the passenger side. "Sir, do you have any other form of identification? There appears to be a problem with your license." The man kept smiling.

"Sorry, that is all I have," he said.

"Do you have a credit card with your name on it?" asked the trooper.

"No, I always pay in cash."

"Sir, please step out of the car."

"Why?" asked the man. Surely there is some kind of mistake. Maybe we could work something out." Ramirez's smile disappeared. Trying to bride of state trooper over a ticket was either stupid or the act of a desperate person. This man did not look stupid.

"Sir, please exit the vehicle now. Do not make this worse than it has to be." Ramirez's voice left no room for discussion. "Without a valid license, you are under arrest. Step out of the vehicle." Ramirez knew his body camera would catch the bribe attempt. He also knew it was not a good case. The man looked at Ramirez and then at the deputy. The deputy had his hand on his pistol. This was not the time to fight. Pay a quick fine and be on his way. The man slowly exited the vehicle with his hands up. Ramirez turned him around and handcuffed him.

"Is that really necessary?" he asked.

"It is for your safety and mine." Ramirez and the deputy walked the man back to the trooper's vehicle. The man was placed in the second row of seats. These seats were enclosed by metal shielding to make sure no one left the vehicle on their own. Ramirez looked at the deputy, "Can you please watch him while I check the car?" "No problem," said the deputy. Ramirez inventoried the vehicle and found nothing suspicious. Ramirez thanked the deputy and said he would wait for the tow truck. He could start his paperwork. The deputy left, and Ramirez read the man his rights, which many call the Miranda warning, because the court case that required the warning came from the arrest of Ernest Miranda in Arizona. At this point, the man stopped talking and would not acknowledge the rights that were read. A few minutes later, a tow truck arrived to take the vehicle to the police impound lot. As soon as the truck left, Ramirez pulled out into traffic and headed for the jail.

When he got to the jail, Ramirez secured his weapon and ammo. Even a trooper could not bring these items into a jail. He walked the man into the jail. While one jailer removed the handcuffs and did another search of the man, Ramirez spoke to the intake jailer.

"What do you have, trooper?" asked the senior corrections officer.

"I am not sure. Started with speeding, has a phony driver's license, and is too relaxed for what is going on. Can you run his fingerprints for me, nationwide, while I do my paperwork?"

"No problem, think he is a big bad guy?" joked the corrections officer.

"Not sure, something is not right. I will be at the table doing my paperwork. Besides traffic, I have him for a phony state document and maybe an attempted bride, maybe." Ramirez sat down and started all the paperwork you never see on television.

The man was escorted by another corrections officer to the main desk. There, all his property was itemized, and he was asked if he needed medical attention. He did not answer. When the corrections officer attempted to fingerprint the man, the fight was on. Two other corrections officers joined the wrestling match. It ended quickly with no one being noticeably injured. The fingerprints were obtained, and the thought of adding another charge was considered. Rameriz was about halfway through his paperwork when the senior corrections officer yelled, "Holy Crap." Ramirez got up to see what was wrong. "You hooked a whale," said the corrections officer. They both looked at the computer screen. There was the man's face, his height and weight, hair and eye color, and a warrant from the Drug Enforcement Agency for international narcotics smuggling and another from Homeland Security for murder. No bail would be allowed.

"Are you sure?" asked Ramirez.

"Yep, sure am, even confirmed the scar on his leg. It is him."

Ramirez got on his phone to call his sergeant and let him know he would be running late today. The sergeant said it would not be a problem. "Take your time, do it right." The corrections officer called the phone number on the warrant screen. After assuring them that it was not a joke and the identification was confirmed, the officer was told someone from the DEA and DHS would be there shortly. Under no circumstances could the man make bail or be released. They would wait for the Feds to arrive and explain what was going on.

After about twenty minutes, 2 men in suits and three men in tactical gear entered the jail. They identified themselves as DEA and DHS Special Agents. The men in tactical clothing remained silent.

"Are you the officer who made the arrest?" asked one of them.

"I am State Trooper Ramirez, and yes, I made the arrest. He was speeding and showed a fake driver's license."

"I am DEA Special Agent Wilson. I am the DEA supervisor for the El Paso area. This is DHS Special Agent Jackson, my counterpart in this part of Texas." Jackson nodded but said nothing. "The man you arrested is Antonio Gonzalez, the number 2 man for all narcotics in this part of Texas and Northern Mexico. Both the US and Mexico have rewards out for him totaling in the millions.

"Too bad you can't collect," said Wilson.

"Who is number one?" asked Ramirez. "The number one man is his father, Rafael Gonzalez. He has an even bigger reward for his capture," said Jackson. "These men will take the prisoner off your hands. He is facing the death penalty on Federal charges."

"Well," said Ramirez, "that beats my speeding ticket."

"Expect a letter of commendation from either Justice or DHS, you took a dangerous man off the streets," Wilson said.

Ramirez smiled, "That is why I make the big bucks." Everyone knew the trooper made a lot less than the guys in suits.

The three men in tactical gear searched Gonzalez. They placed the leather security belt around his waist and handcuffed each hand separately to the belt. They also put a shock belt around his waist. The agents could press a button, and a non-lethal, but very painful jolt of electricity would encompass Gonzalez's waist. They finished by putting shackles on his feet. He would barely walk, let alone run. This prisoner was cunning and had murdered several people. The agents would take no chances. The agents and the prisoner left the jail. Then entered an unmarked black van. There were no windows except for the driver's and the front passenger's. They headed for the nearest federal jail facility. Ramirez finished his paperwork and headed home. The two hours of overtime pay would be used to take his family to dinner.

Chapter Fifteen

Rafael Gonzalez was sitting at home when the call came. To call the 6,000+ square foot house a home did it no credit. An Olympic pool and tennis courts did not get in the way of his huge circular driveway. At any time, there would be sports cars, SUVs, and luxury sedans. Life was good. He had more money than he or his children could ever spend. Still, he wanted more. Besides being in charge of all narcotics operations in this part of Mexico, he also controlled human trafficking. His other businesses did not bring in the hundreds of millions that his two main businesses brought in. The only thing he loved more than money was his son, his firstborn. Cancer took his beloved wife. All his wealth and connections could not save her. Now it was just him and his son, Antonio. His son would inherit the business when he was gone. That time was not now. He fought his way up to be the regional boss. No one would dare challenge him. The ground held many that did.

The call was from one of his many lawyers in El Paso. Antonio had been stopped for speeding and had been arrested. The American Federal police had him now. No bail was allowed. He was being held in solitary confinement, with only his lawyer being allowed to see him. The lawyer had already filed papers with the court to have Antonio released on bail. Any bail could be met. The lawyer would hear back from the judge in a few hours. The lawyer knew this judge; she could not be bought or scared. They had already assigned three U. S.

Marshals to guard her. There were also two Marshals outside of Antonio's cell. There was no way to get anything to him. Even the lawyer was searched before going into the cell. They charged him with a variety of charges. It was the murder charge and the narcotics trafficking charge that would be the biggest problems. One carried the death penalty, the other life without parole. The lawyer already filed paperwork to see all the evidence against his client. The lawyer would call Rafael as soon as anything was discovered. "Call me anytime, day or night, no delays," screamed Rafael.

Rafael was angry beyond words. He repeatedly told his son not to go into the United States. Here in Mexico, he had power, money, and connections. His son and his business were safe. Lately in the U.S., law enforcement had been hunting for his "employees" with vigor. The American warrants would never be served in Mexico. Now he hoped his lawyer could do something quickly. The days of bribery and intimidation were coming to an end. He picked up his television remote and turned on his huge flatscreen TV. Thanks to the huge satellite dish on his roof, he could watch television from almost anywhere. With some hesitation, he clicked the remote for an El Paso channel. The news was talking about a multi-car pileup on Interstate 10. The road had been closed to traffic, and cars were backed up for over a mile already. It was unknown how many people were hurt or killed. This was of little interest to him. He left the screen on and reviewed paperwork showing his profits from his different businesses.

Of course, the business names were phony. Anyone who did not know might think these were normal business reports. Rafael knew better and knew what they really meant. Tens of millions of dollars in profit. Just then, a reporter broke in to story on the accident. "We interpret our broadcast with a breaking news. The Department of Homeland Security has announced the arrest of Antonio Gonzalez, the second most wanted person in the area. Gonzalez was charged with murder and various narcotics charges. His lawyer said the charges are ridiculous and would be addressed in court. Gonzalez is now in a maximum security prison. Bail was denied."

Rafael shook his head and yelled, "No" at the top of his lungs. A guard who was outside Rafael's office rushed in. "Get out," screamed Rafael. Just then, the telephone rang. It was his lawyer.

"The judge ruled against us. There must be pressure from Washington. They will not deal, and they are still seeking the death penalty."

Rafael fought back the rage. Even with all his power and wealth, his son was beyond his reach.

"Do they have a case against my son?"

"I am sorry to say they do. There are witnesses and video of him killing the undercover DEA agent. He even bragged about it on a phone call they were listening to. They have the recording. I do not see a way of getting him out of this." Rafael grew livid.

"Bribe whoever you have to, open a contract on the witnesses. Do whatever must be done. Bring my son home." He slammed the phone down. "My son, my son," he cried. Rafael sat alone in the room for hours.

Several weeks later, Rafael realized that his efforts had accomplished nothing. Witnesses were protected by US Marshals. They were moved every other day. The video evidence was secured. An attempt to bribe one of the property managers who safeguarded the evidence led to the arrest of one of his men. That didn't matter to Rafael. All efforts had failed. There must be something. He called a meeting of his top lieutenants. Maybe one of them would have an idea. They came from all over Northern Mexico. They were man who dealt in death and narcotics, in human trafficking and prostitution. They kept their hands clean; others did their dirty work. It looked like a corporate board meeting. In many ways, it was.

"You all know why you are here," said Rafael. "You know about my son's problems and my efforts to help him. I need your advice and help. We have known each other for many years. I ask you as a friend and a father for your ideas."

"Is there any way to threaten the family of one of the Marshals? He could be "convinced" to look the other way?" came the first answer.

"No, there are always at least two Marshals there with him at any one time," said Rafael. "Trying to get to two Marshals at the same time is impossible. They rotate assignments. It is never the same two Marshals at any one time." The room went quiet.

"There is no way to attack the prison; it is too well guarded," came another comment. "I know that, don't you think I thought of that already?" Rafael boomed. Once again, the room went quiet. They sat there for several minutes. Then Carlos Ortega, the man who controlled the area north of Mexico City all the way to the Texas border, smiled.

"We trade, we give them something they want more than your son for his release." Everyone looked at him.

"What do we have that they want more than my son?" asked Rafael.

"We give them information," smiled Ortega.

The room went silent. Rafael asked slowly, "What are you talking about?"

"I have some property north of Mexico City. I "rented it out" to some Iranian businessman. He used it to train some "freedom fighters." They are going to make a major attack on the United States. I figured after the attack, there would be a greater demand for our product. He paid a very high price for room and board," Ortega smiled.

"You did what? Without asking me first. Are you mad? If it ever came back on us, the Americans would invade Mexico and bomb all our manufacturing centers. You know their satellites fly overhead," screamed Rafael. Ortega shrank back into his seat. Rafael considered shooting him right there. To do something this big, without asking first. Ortega would be dealt with very soon, but first. "You will give me everything you have or know about these people. Pictures, documents, travel plans, anything!" screamed Rafael. "You will have it all here in 24 hours, or I will make some permanent changes to the leadership in your area. Every one of your people who had contact with any of these foreigners will be here tomorrow. You are on very thin ice; do not make me raise my voice again, or it will be the last you ever hear." Ortega nodded his head quickly. He had not known fear since he was a young man working the streets of Mexico City. Now he knew fear again and didn't like it. The meeting ended. Ortega went into the hallway and called his people. He left no room for doubt that all his people would comply with Rafael's orders. They would be here with all the information demanded. Once alone, Rafael called his lawyer.

The lawyer answered on the second ring. "I have an important job for you. Call the American Attorney General immediately. Tell him there will be a major terrorist attack on the United States in the next few weeks. Ask them how valuable this information is. Specifically, enough to deport my son."

The line was quiet; the lawyer was dumbfounded. "Boss, you are playing with fire. Suppose they think you are part of this plot. There will be paratroopers in your backyard within a day."

"You told me they have a solid case against my son. They want to execute him. You can not get him freed. What choice do I have? Tell the AG I just found out about this within the hour." The lawyer breathed slowly and deeply. He would make the call. Before he did, he whispered a prayer.

The United States Attorney General had just walked into his office when one of his deputies came running in. Yes, he was actually running. AG Thompson looked up in amazement. He had never seen this man excited before. The deputy had handled big cases and never even blinked. Now there was a look of panic on his face. This would have to be something really big.

Chapter Sixteen

"Sir, we just had a telephone call from the lawyer representing Rafael Gonzalez," said the deputy.

"Is he surrendering?" asked the AG.

"No, sir, he wants to swap information about an upcoming terrorist attack on the U.S. for the deportation of his son."

"What the hell?" said the AG. "Are you kidding me? His son is number two on the most wanted list. He was legally arrested and is in federal custody. He is a cop killer."

"Yes, sir, I know," said the deputy. "He claims that there will be a major terrorist attack on the US within a week or so. He can provide photos of the men and their destinations." "Destinations, plural? asked the AG.

"Sir, if you believe what he is saying, there will be 50 attacks at the same time."

"Oh my," the AG could not get the words out.

"Get me the Director of Homeland Security on the secure phone now! Get me the deputy AG in El Paso on the phone. I need to call the DNI," said the AG. Within a minute, his phone rang. "DHS Director Good on the phone for you, sir."

"Phil, this is Tom."

"What can I do for you, Tom?" asked the DHS Director. The AG told him about the events of the last few minutes.

"Can this be true?"

"I do not know, but my next call is to the DNI. Please start getting your staff ready. After the DNI, my next call is to the President."

The AG called the Director of National Intelligence on the secure line. He had no knowledge of the attack. The last major event was some cargo ship carrying arms mixing it up with a Navy destroyer. The Navy won. Since then, everything has been quiet. "This has something to do with Mexico, but I do not know what. Our most wanted criminal will provide the information, if we deport his son, our number two on the list, and a cop killer," said the AG. "OK, I have to call the President. Keep in touch," said the AG.

The AG called the White House. There were public phone numbers. There were also private telephone numbers that would get the caller through most, but not all, of the screeners. The President's time was very tightly monitored.

"I had a major emergency and need to talk to the President immediately," said the AG. Within a minute, a voice came on the line.

"Tom, what can I do for you?" came the President's voice.

The AG told the President all he knew. "I have also alerted the DNI and the DHS Director. They have no knowledge of anything going on." The President was quiet for a few moments.

"What do you recommend, Tom?"

"Mr. President, I would hate to release this cop killer and drug smuggler. I am not sure how we can confirm the story. Still, if we do nothing and the attack occurs, well, it would be totally unacceptable."

The President asked, "How long before you can be here?" "20 to 30 minutes, Mr. President, depending on traffic," answered the AG. "Get here, I'll call the others."

"Yes, Mr. President, answered the AG.

The meeting started 35 minutes later. The President welcomed his AG, the DHS Director, the Director of the FBI, the Secretary of State, the DNI, and the Deputy Secretary of War. The actual Secretary was in the Pacific area, visiting the troops.

The President started the meeting. "Ladies and gentlemen, we are here because the AG has brought up a problem, and I need your help solving it." The President then explained what was known about the situation. The DNI said he had no information about any such threat. The Director of Homeland Security said the same. The FBI Director also had no information, but could mobilize his agents within an hour. The Deputy Secretary of War said, "We have no intelligence on this. I can activate numerous forces with the hour, but we may run into a legal problem operating troops in our cities."

"What about a raid into Mexico to capture this guy?" asked the Secretary of State.

"It wouldn't work, for a few reasons," said the Deputy Secretary of War. "We do not have the time to plan the operation properly. We have no information about the layout of the home, nor its defenses. This character is probably armed and has lots of security, based on his line of work. We would have to go in hard with paratroopers or Marines. This would lead to loss of life on both sides, an international incident, and we might wind up killing him."

The room was quiet for a few moments. The AG joined in, "I do not want to give this kid a free pass and get nothing in exchange. How can we confirm the information and its value without letting him free?"

The Secretary of State said, "I have an idea." All heads turned towards him. How about if we promise, in writing, to deport his son to Mexico after we confirm the information and it proves to be actionable? If the attack goes forth, his son faces lethal injection for killing the DEA agent. Even if we let him go, we might get him in the future."

Once again, the room went quiet. Then the President spoke up. "AG, call his lawyer, set up a meeting on U.S. soil. If his information leads to the successful stopping of the attack, we will release and deport his son. This is not amnesty. Just a one-time "get out of jail free card." If the father is jerking us around, let him know his son's trial will be quick and efficient. Take some folks with you from the DNI's office, as well as DHS agents. If this is real, we need to know ASAP. If he is blowing smoke, make sure he knows he poked the wrong bear."

The meeting adjourned, and the key players went back to their offices as fast as the traffic would allow. They did not have red lights and sirens like the President. Once back at their offices, the phone lines lit up. Organizations were being mobilized, but for what?

The AG called Rafael's lawyer. A plan was made to meet the next day. If the intelligence prevented a major terrorist attack, his son would be deported to Mexico and would not be allowed reentry. The meeting would be held in Mexico, at Rafael's home. There, the Americans could review the videos and question anyone they wanted to. Rafael gave his personal guarantee for their safety. If anything happened to any member of the US group, there would be hell to pay. Rafael assured them he wanted his son back and the attack would hurt his business. He gave the coordinates of his home. His runway could accommodate light aircraft and helicopters.

The American group was made up of the Attorney General, an assistant secretary of state for Latin America, a senior operations officer from DHS, a senior member of the FBI, and several members of JITF-CT. JITF-CT was the Joint Intelligence Task Force for Counter Terrorism. This highly professional, but little-known organization was the War Department hub for counter terrorism. Not spies nor commandos, they were the most educated intelligence types in their field. Everyone boarded an Air Force plane at Joint Base Andrews and headed to El Paso. The flight was long and silent. If true, they had only days to stop a major terrorist attack.

The C-17 landed at Biggs Field in El Paso. This field is adjacent to Fort Bliss. The group exited the aircraft. No time to rest. The group boarded two V-22 Osprey aircraft. This aircraft can take off vertically and then fly forward. The propeller cells on the end of the wing can pivot from vertical to straight forward. The group was divided in half. This was in case of an aircraft crash or attack. The group could not be destroyed so easily. As the Ospreys started to take off, two infantry platoons took off in two CH-47 Chinooks helicopters. The four aircraft were followed by four Apache gunships. The group would not enter Mexico unarmed and unprotected. Rafael assured them that the Mexican government would not object. Rafael had many friends in the government.

The flight took less than an hour. No one would appreciate the beauty of the Mexican scenery. The soldiers were worried about flying into a foreign country armed. The executive group worried about the validity of the terrorist claim; could they trust Rafael, and if true, what could they do about it? It was a very tense flight. The pilots flew directly to the coordinates given. If this were a trap, it would serve little purpose. The escorting aircraft would destroy the compound and everyone in it. First, the Chinooks landed. The infantry platoons exited the aircraft the second the wheels touched the ground. They set up a perimeter around the runway. The Ospreys landed next. The executive group exited the rear ramp onto the runway. The Apache helicopters circled the runway. This let them observe what was happening on the ground. They would stay overhead until they got the signal to land. If they were given the distress signal, the Apache helicopter would rain fire and death on everyone and everything. It would mean the executive group was being captured or worse. There would be no hostages.

Their worst fears never came to pass. Rafael met the group on the runway. He was unarmed and wearing a tailored suit. He looked like the perfect host. "Ladies and gentlemen, welcome to my home. While you are here, you are under my protection. I understand why you feel the need for all this security, but I assure you it is not necessary." The group looked around. There were no visible weapons, and the few men standing near Rafael were neatly dressed and looked relaxed. The four Apache helicopters circling overhead did not seem to bother them. Rafael showed the group the way into his home. One platoon of infantry went into the home to make sure there were no surprises. The other platoon remained outside guarding the parked aircraft.

"Welcome to my home," said Rafael. It was a huge house. There was obviously a second level, based on the long stairway that rose at least 40 feet to what looked like an entertainment room. They had no idea of how many bedrooms were up there. The group had seen the pool, tennis court, and stables from the air. "Would you like a drink, some tea?"

The AG answered, "No, thank you. We are not here to socialize. I would like to do our business and leave."

"I understand," said Rafael. "Please follow me to the conference room."

The group followed Rafael. The infantry platoon leader placed himself between Rafael and the American group. At the first sign of trouble, he would shoot Rafael. No hesitation, just shoot the most wanted man in America. Rafael and the group took seats around a large wooden table. It was so highly polished that you could see yourself in the reflection. The soldiers remained standing. They spread around the room, but not in front of any of the large windows. There might be snipers. All the soldiers were in full combat gear. They looked out of place in this huge room. The infantry lieutenant thought to himself that he had never seen so many books outside of a library. Floor to ceiling, around the room.

"May I offer you a drink or some food?" said Rafael, always the proper host.

"No, thank you, can we just conduct business and be done with this?" said the AG. He was not about to sit and chit-chat with the most wanted man in the U.S.

"Very well, right to business. Here is what I want, and here is what I am offering. I want my son back with me in Mexico. I know you have a strong case against him and you want him dead." Rafael paused. "My son is very important to me. We will not discuss his crimes and shortcomings. We all know he has done terrible things." There was many nodding of heads around the table. Antonio's list of crimes was very long. Those were just the ones that the U.S. government knew about.

"Here is what I am offering in exchange. It has come to my attention that an Iranian national has 50 suicide bombers that he has sent to the US to attack your country very soon. The attack will be spread throughout your country. I will provide photos of the bombers, their targets, and the time of their attacks." The room went totally silent. Everyone from the AG to the lowest ranking solider was stunned. Fifty attacks at one time. The room remained silent for a few moments.

The FBI representative asked, "How did you come by this information, and how reliable is it?" Rafael looked a bit uncomfortable.

"A member of my organization decided to make some money without my knowledge and consent. I do not allow such dealings. You know what I have done, and terrorism is not one of them. He rented out his estate to the leader of this group and the fifty people who would do the actual attack. While these people were at the estate, my former employee took pictures of the terrorists and listened to their planning."

The FBI agent said, "I would like to question him personally."

Rafael shook his head, "That will not be possible."

"Why not?" asked the FBI agent.

"You must understand what he did was against my wishes and could bring considered focus on me and my dealings. I could not allow his conduct to be overlooked."

"You killed him?"

Rafael smiled, "I never said that. Besides, your US laws have no bearing in Mexico. Let us just say he will never trouble your country again, ever!"

Once again, the room was silent. "We cannot release your son until we know the information is accurate and actionable. The saving of numerous American lives would be more important than the life of your son to us," said the AG. Rafael winced at the "life of your son" comment. "With the source of this information being 'unavailable,' determining its accuracy would be difficult." "I assure you, Mr. Attorney General, the source was very forthcoming to me," said Rafael.

The AG looked around the room. "May we have some privacy to discuss the issue?"

"Of course." Said Rafael.

"One question before you leave," asked the JITF-CT representative, "as a sign of good faith, when is the attack planned for?"

Rafael paused, thought a moment, and smiled, "On the 4th of July."

"The 4th of July, son of a bitch," yelled the FBI representative. That is less than a week away. Fifty targets to identify and stop. Is that even possible?"

"Do we have a choice?" said the AG

The DHS representative joined in. "DHS and the FBI have folks in every state. We can mobilize state and local cops. The Marshals are very good at finding people. We need to do a full court press and do it now."

"We need to know who to look for. Not only a name and face, but where are they going?" said the FBI representative.

"We need to make the deal, but carefully," muttered the AG. "Anyone have an issue with the deal? Speak up now." Everyone looked around the room. No one wanted to speak first and help to release a cop killer. They had no choice.

The AG opened the door and told the man standing outside, obviously security, to get Rafael. The man walked away quickly. "OK, we will make this deal, but with some safety measures," said the AG. Rafael walked into the room. He sat at the table. "Mr. Gonzalez, I will make you this promise. If your information is accurate and actionable, I will have your son deported to Mexico. He will be banned from returning to the United States. The current criminal charges against him will remain. I know Mexico will not extradite him to the United States due to the pending death penalty. Now, the other side of the coin. If this information is false or a diversion, you and your son will be reclassified as enemy combatants and not just criminals. You will be the target of both law enforcement and the American military. I think you know what that means."

Rafael smiled and nodded his head. "That is satisfactory."

An aide to the AG wrote out the agreement in two copies. The AG looked at Rafael, "We will both sign it. Two of these senior Americans will cosign as witnesses. We will both keep a copy. Do you agree?"

Rafael said he agreed but asked, "When will my son be released?"

"Within 7 days of the successful completion of this operation," Rafael said that was agreeable.

Rafael called, and a man entered the room. He was carrying two large manila envelopes. Rafael spoke, "The contents of each envelope is the same. There are photos of the 50 terrorists. They never used names while in Mexico. They were called by numbers. The numbers ranged from one to fifty. The man in charge of this is Mohammad Abu al-Fadi of Bandar Abbas, Iran. He never said why he was funding this action. The targets will be a shopping mall in the capital of each of your states. They would attack the largest mall in each capital. The name of the exact target was never mentioned. They were given their target in a sealed envelope." The American group sat there dumbfounded. This was incredible. Rafael continued, "To make this worse, from your point of view, is that all 50 attacks will take place at the same time on the 4th of July.

"What time is the attack?" asked the DHS representative.

"The attack in Hawaii will take place at noon. That will be at 5 PM in Maine. Each terrorist will throw one hand grenade into a crowd and then walk into another crowd and blow themselves up."

"Oh my God," said the FBI representative. "How do we stop this?"

Rafael shook his head, "I have no idea."

"What weapons are they equipped with?" asked the AG.

"No firearms, just the two grenades each. That would make it easier to transport. They entered the US from two border crossings in

Texas. From there, I have no idea." The group sat silent for a few moments.

As soon as the two documents were signed, the American group boarded the waiting Ospreys. As soon as they lifted off, the two infantry platoons boarded the Chinooks and fell in behind the Ospreys. The four Apache helicopters, which had landed one at a time, had been refueled from bladders kept in the Chinooks. As the Chinooks left the area, the four Apache helicopters took up positions in front and the rear of the Chinooks. They could not keep up with the Ospreys. The AG walked into the cockpit of the Osprey. "Call ahead. When we land, I want transportation to a room with numerous secure phones. I am setting up a temporary command post there." The pilot nodded and made the call.

The Ospreys landed back at Biggs Field. The roar of the rotors was deafening. The tailgate ramp dropped, and the senior American officials walked quickly down the ramp and onto the waiting bus. The bus left the runway as soon as the last official sat down in the bus. It would be at least another half hour before the escort helicopters got back to Biggs.

The bus stopped in front of an unremarkable building. The group exited the bus and entered the building. There was a large room. It had a dozen desks. Each desk had a secure telephone, a normal landline phone, and a secure computer. An Army colonel, Stephens, met the group as they entered. He showed them to their desks. "If you need anything else, please let me know." The AG thanked the colonel for the short-notice preparation. The FBI official asked for coffee and food. The AG gave him a look. The colonel said he would order some as soon as the command post was up and running. The AG thanked the colonel again.

The AG was on the secure phone to the White House immediately. The phone was answered on the first ring. "I need the President now. It doesn't matter what he is doing, now, please." Within a minute, the President was on the phone. The AG told him everything that had happened in Mexico and the information received. There was a pause as the President comprehended everything.

"Tom, you are in charge of this. I want every government agent put on this. I will have the Chairman put the military on alert. They may be able to help with transportation, supplies, or something. I will green-light tier 1 operations on US soil. I will have to let someone in Congress know. I will contact all 50 governors. I want their help with state and local police agencies. Do we have any idea what happens if the terrorists learn that we know?"

"No idea, Mr. President. They know they are going to die, so fear of capture is not something they might worry about. Killing some military personnel or law enforcement will not bother them."

"Tom, until this is over, I will be here, next to the phone. If you need anything, just ask."

"Thank you, Mr. President. I will do my best."

"Do better, Tom. This could have long-lasting consequences for the entire country," said the President.

Colonel Stephens came back into the room. "I have ordered some secure video teleconference devices to be installed. Might take an hour or so, but you will be able to see and hear anyone with a similar device. All major military units have them. Most state governments do not. I am having a direct phone line installed. It will contact me at the office or in my quarters. It is also linked to my cell phone if I am not at either place. Just pick up the phone, no need to dial. I have also secured a building next door. It will have beds and shower facilities for this group. There is a set of toilets in both buildings. There will be guards around both buildings 24/7. If you would, can you make me a list of those here? If they are not on the list, the guards will not allow them to enter. Deadly force is authorized to stop an intruder." Once again, the AG thanked the colonel for his attention to detail.

The folks from JITF-CT had already sent a set of the photographs electronically of the terrorists back to the Defense Intelligence Agency in Washington, D.C. It was hoped that they might be identified. They would be using false names and papers, but there is rarely too much information available. Also, the name and home of the leader of this attack was forwarded to all the major intelligence agencies. The National Reconnaissance Office was tasked to provide imagery for the home and workplace of Mohammad Abu al-Fadi of

Bandar Abbas, Iran. That information would no doubt be needed when the threat had been neutralized.

The AG stood up and called for their attention. "As I see it, we have several tasks. We must identify these terrorists. We must identify their targets. Finally, we must deploy forces, regardless of which agency, to stop these attacks. There will be no glory hounds here. We are one team defending one country."

"I want a map or photo of every state capitol. All major malls will be highlighted. We do not have enough people to cover every mall in America at the same time. I want a floor plan of every mall. I want all the border crossing videos from Texas in the last week. Someone will need to go through every frame of video and see when and where these people came into the country. Once the vehicle is identified, use any means necessary to follow the vehicle and see where it went. AS these people go to different states, we must follow them." The AG took a breath. The FBI representative jumped in.

"Since we know where they are going, why don't we concentrate our resources and time there?"

"If we can stop them before they get to a crowded area, I think that would be better. However, you are right, the majority of our people should be at the malls, "said the AG.

Within an hour, a map of every capital was printed out and posted on the walls of the workspace. They were posted in order of statehood. It was a safe guess that with 50 terrorists going to 50 states, the numbers related to which state came first. This was the easy part. Then, malls had to be identified. Some capital cities only had one main mall. Others had more. Each one would have to be protected. The number of people in the building grew. The bosses left, and the workers did the actual analysis. The main room got noisier and more crowded. The AG remained behind to coordinate. Customs and Border Protection electronically sent the videos of border crossings in Texas for the last week. Intelligence analysis went over each frame of video and compared them to the pictures of the terrorists they had gotten from Rafael. More analysis from the 1st Armored Division arrived. Intelligent personnel from Battalion to Division level arrived at Biggs Field to help. Even though they all had Top Secret security clearances, they were still sworn to secrecy by the AG personally. They worked around the clock to assist in identifying the routes the terrorist took and what their likely target might be.

The President started calling governors. Calling 50 governors was a huge task. The Vice President was told to start calling, also. Each governor was told there was a serious terrorist threat to a mall in the state capitol on the 4th of July. Even the time of the attack could be given. The President did not want anyone to leak this information, cause a panic, and maybe cause the terrorists to attack another target. The governors were not told that this was a nationwide attack. Each was made aware of what would happen to them if they leaked this.

Each governor said they understood and would take steps to contain the situation. The governors were also told that they would have federal agents at the malls to assist. Intelligence updates would be provided as they came in. They were wished well. The President sat back in his large padded chair. He was exhausted, and he knew things were just beginning.

Chapter Seventeen

As the command group at Briggs Field continued to go over the border video, they also reviewed camera videos along the Texas highway and transportation hubs in south and southeast Texas. The buses which came across at the border were, of course, filmed. The analysists worked hard to identify which terrorists were in which bus. It was not clear in many cases. However, the vehicle and its license plate were clear, and this was compared to other cameras throughout the state. The vehicles were tracked to San Antonio and Corpus Christi, Texas. The buses dropped men off at the train station and the bus depot. Their faces were not always clear. The number of men added up to 48. Where were the other two terrorists?

#49 had been on a freighter heading for Juneau, Alaska, for several days. Even in the summertime, the weather felt cold to a man who had lived his entire life in the desert. Deserts do get cold at night, but they do not rock from the waves. Standing on the deck, there was always a cold wind, sometimes accompanied by cold sea spray. He did not mind dying for his beliefs, but freezing to death was almost more than he could handle.

#50 was also on a freighter. He would reach Honolulu the day after next. The sun was warm, and the seas were calm. He was enjoying his last week on earth. He had heard about Hawaii, and now he would see it, for a day or so. He had little to do, so he sat in the sunshine and reflected on the glory of killing so many infidels. The perfect end to a glorious trip.

The FBI showed up in force in both San Antonio and Corpus Christi. They questioned everyone connected to the bus lines and the train system. Several people remembered a few of the terrorists. They were quiet and never together with anyone else. No one could remember exactly where they were headed to. It had been a couple of days, and with the vast number of passengers, they did not stand out. There had been buses and trains going all over the country. Of course, they could go to one city and then change trains or buses to go elsewhere. It was an impossible task. All video recordings were taken and sent to the FBI in Quantico, Virginia. There, scientists and criminologists would review every moment of video for any clues. Time was running out, and they were nowhere.

Back at Biggs Field, the intelligence people were reviewing each state capitol for possible targets. In some states, the choice was easy if the information from Rafael was accurate. However, there were some capitols that had more than one possible target. Each selection was reviewed by Sergeant Major Rogers. Rogers was the command sergeant major for the Armored Division's G-2 or staff intelligence office. He had almost 30 years of experience in the intelligence field. He started as an intelligence clerk in a front-line armored cavalry squadron. He worked his way up, seeing combat several times. He knew the cost of bad intelligence. It was blood. "Let's go, people.

There are hundreds of federal agents and local police waiting on this. They need time to plan, also." Rogers' boss, Lieutenant Colonel Jeff Miller, was the G-2. He was the head intelligence officer for the Division. He knew his people, and he knew Rogers. He watched Rogers supervise and check the work being done. He would not micromanage his sergeant major. He was there to keep other agencies from interfering with their work. Considering the information they were given and the time it took to set up the intelligence cell, they were doing a great job. The brass would not let them work out of their own offices. No, they had to set up in the command post building. Nearer to the brass. That sounded good, but they also had to move all their equipment and materials to the new building. This took time. There were always these high ranking civilian butting in and slowing down the analysis. Miller had spoken to his boss, the Division Commander. "Please get these guys out of my hair. I have to field the same questions over and over again." The two-star general smiled. Not even his rank could make this group of civilians back off.

The executive group met daily at 0600, 1200, and 1800. The workers worked while they slept at night. Sergeant Major Rogers was getting ready to brief them, and the information he had would not be to their liking. He took a deep breath and headed to the front of the room. Lieutenant Colonel Miller got in his way.

"Sergeant Major, I know what you are going to say, and I know how it will be received. I'll take the hit."

"But, Sir," the Sergeant Major snapped back, "They can't hurt me. I've got my 30, just about, and there is no way I can be promoted. You don't even have 20 and can still advance."

"All true," said Miller, "But this is why I get the big bucks."

Miller refused the briefing notes and walked to the front of the room. "Ladies and Gentlemen, may I have your attention please?" All heads turned to Miller. They were hoping for some "magic bullet" which would solve their problems. Miller did not have it. "Folks, we have had numerous members of the Armed Forces, the Intelligence Community, and Federal Law Enforcement working this problem around the clock since you brought it here. It is now July 1st and we are no closer to answering the important questions." The room got very still. "We have identified a few of the terrorists, but believe this information is useless as they are traveling under false identification. Putting their real names into the computer system would get us nothing. The FBI has checked every train and bus that they could. There are so many combinations that finding how they got to their destinations is impossible. At least one and probably two have traveled by ship. The person behind this attack has numerous connections in the shipping industry. It would not be a problem to get the terrorist to Hawaii and Alaska unseen. As they are carrying hand grenades, it is extremely doubtful that they traveled by air. Number #49 has probably not driven to Alaska, as it would have taken too long, and our Canadian neighbors have little humor when it comes to bringing explosives into their country. We must attack the problem in another way."

"We have their pictures and a pretty good idea of their targets. We know the date and time of the attack. I recommend that law enforcement, not the military, engage these targets. Cops, federal or local, can walk the malls on the 4th. We can provide the photos of the suspects to all agencies. We know they work alone, so law enforcement can ID and stop them, using whatever method is best for the situation. I do not think a strong unconfirmed presence is wise. It might cause the terrorist to attack earlier or just go somewhere else. I know it is a gamble, but I think the best option is to let them enter the mall and then stop them. Closing the mall or posting a bunch of uniforms will make us lose what little control of the situation we have." Miller stopped and took a breath. "Oh well, there goes my career," he thought to himself.

The room was quiet for a moment. Then it erupted in yelling. "We can't just do nothing and wait," said the FBI representative. "We can have agents in every capital by tomorrow," said the DHS representative. The JITF-CT team knew Miller was right and started to prepare photo pack files that could be sent instantly to anyone by email. They were ready to alert any and every agency that needed the information.

"Colonel, can you give us a few minutes, please?" asked the AG.

"Yes, Sir," Miller responded. As Miller and Rogers left the room, Miller saw the general standing quietly in the corner of the room. He did not know the general was there for the briefing. The general smiled at Miller and gave him a thumbs-up hand gesture. Okay, maybe his career was not over.

As soon as Miller, Rogers, and the general left the room, chaos erupted. Everyone had an idea. No one liked the other agency's idea. Most did not like the idea of having the terrorists come to them. No one wanted to wait. The Attorney General stood up and yelled, "Quiet." The room settled down. "Look, I do not like sitting around and waiting to be attacked either. But, and this is a big but, we do not know how these assholes are coming to our capitols. We know who, by face only, we know when, and are pretty sure we know where. We only have 2 days to stop them. I wish there were a better plan, but I think we should go with the deployment of law enforcement to the malls. Not just federal, but state and local also. All in plain clothes and ready to stop the attack. These terrorists are not going to respond to "de-escalation techniques" or community relations types. They will need to be stopped and stopped hard." The FBI representative started to say something about the liability of just shooting the terrorist when the AG cut him off. "You work for me, and I say we stop them. Once the pin on the grenade was pulled and the lever or "spoon" was released, there was no way to stop the explosion. I want FBI, U.S. Marshals, DHS agents, state troopers, and local law enforcement in the malls. They will act casual and look like any other shopper. Their job will be to identify the terrorists before they strike and stop them. We owe the American people that. We will contact the governor of each state and the police chief of the city concerned and alert them. Do it now!" said the AG in a loud voice. There would be no arguments.

Chapter Eighteen

#50 stood on the bow of the ship as it approached Honolulu. The ship's captain told him they would be docking near Sand Island and very close to the old cultural center. As the ship left California and did not go to another country, there would be no customs to go through. There were, of course, police and Border Patrol officers at the docks, but they would not pose a problem. #50 was a bit nervous. He had only been to 2 countries in his life, Iran and Syria. Here, he did not speak the language or know the local customs. His training in Mexico had given him some idea of what to do here. They had docked without incident. True to his word, the local authorities paid him no attention. Just another seaman getting off a ship. He walked through the terminal. There were several cabs waiting there. He got into the first cab. The cab driver asked where he was going. #50 did not understand the words, but knew what he was asking. He handed the cab driver a piece of paper with the name and address of the hotel he had been booked into. They drove east on Ala Moana Boulevard, over the Ala Moana Bridge. There, #50 saw more hotels than he could imagine. They all seemed clean and bright. The cab stopped in front of the hotel. In his instructions, #50 was told how much to pay the driver. Too much or too little would make him easy to remember. The money had no meaning to #50; he would be dead soon.

He walked into the hotel and was stunned. He was told this would be an average hotel. Too upscale might draw attention. A cheap hotel might have more crime and, therefore, more police presence. This "average" hotel was the grandest building he had ever seen. He walked up to the desk and showed his phony passport and credit card. The young lady at the counter smiled and said things he did not understand, but he took to be a warm welcome. Where was her head cover? She was like so many of these infidel women. She would learn soon what it was to be an American. He took the key and took the elevator to his room. Once inside the room, he was again stunned by the size of the room. The large bed and color television. He had never seen a bathroom that big. There were numerous clean towels and all sorts of soaps. If they were not infidels, he could get used to this lifestyle. He opened the curtains and walked out onto the balcony. He looked to his left and saw the mountain they called Diamond Head. It was truly impressive. The Pacific Ocean was in front of him. Water as far as the eye could see. The cool breeze off the ocean was so pleasant. Had he not sworn an oath, he could get used to this. Of course, he only had enough money for a few days. Maybe Mohammad didn't trust them to stay on mission. He would never know.

His target was the Royal Hawaiian Center. His target envelope has a few pictures of it. It was beautiful and sold items from many countries and cultures. It was located at 2201 Kalākaua Ave, a short walk away. Before he died, #50 wanted to sleep in that huge bed and use the facilities of the bathroom.

#49 had just stepped off the small cargo ship in Juneau, Alaska, when it started to rain. It may have been a light rain by Alaskan standards, but for a man from a small town in the center of Iran, this was overwhelming. It was not a warm rain either. He zipped up his coat and turned his collar up. As he walked down the dock, he saw ships of unbelievable size. Some were bigger than his hometown. He was told to expect them, but it was hard to see the entire ship without turning his head. Thousands of tourists came and went on these ships. These people would be his targets.

He did not see a taxi and was forced to walk in the rain. These infidels would pay for this affront. He didn't understand that his deity brought the rain. He walked on for at least six miles until he saw his hotel. He was grateful. He admitted it was very pretty here, so green. He had never seen so much plant life. The mountains were huge compared to what he was used to. He entered the hotel and checked in. The reservation had been made in the name on his fake passport. He went through the lobby to the elevator. Just prior to getting on the elevator, #49 saw a table with numerous fliers about things for tourists to do. Some looked very interesting, but he had no time for that. He did pick up a street map of Juneau. Once inside his room, he took off his wet clothes, took a hot shower, and rested on the bed. The good thing about this hotel was that it was a short walk to his target. He was almost there. Just a short walk up Egan Drive, and he could go to paradise knowing he had killed so many Americans. He looked out the window. It was still raining, only harder now. Hopefully, it would stop before he had to make his final walk.

At the same time, 48 other terrorists made their way to their target cities. Some had an easy time. The West Coast cities were easy due to a lack of security on their buses and trains. Several of the terrorists got some interesting looks in Wyoming and Montana. They stood out no matter where they went. Staying in their hotel room was their only way not to draw attention. The East Coast was fairly simple to get around in.

However, plans never go as planned. When terrorist 4 checked into the Atlanta hotel, he had a problem. Several locals were having a drink or two or more in the hotel bar. While standing at the front desk to check in, the four drunk good old boys were leaving the bar and passed very close to him. They were obviously drunk. Their voices were loud, and at least two of them had trouble walking. They smelled of liquor. "Hey, boy, are you a Mexican?" asked the obviously drunk and overweight man. He was in his mid-20s. 4 could not have any disturbance that would draw attention to himself. He continued to check in by handing his credit card to the young lady behind the desk. The drunk put his hand on 4's shoulder. "Hey, I am talking to you." 4 almost panicked. What could he do? He could not fight them all. He could use the grenade, but that would mean a failed mission. He was about to scream when the lady behind the desk yelled at the four drunk men. "You guys are drunk. Leave now, or I'll call the cops." The loudmouth said something under his breath. He took his hand off of 4's shoulder. The four drunks left the lobby. 4 tried to calm down. He took his room key and headed for his room. He would not leave the room until it was time to go to the mall.

11 had gotten off the bus in Albany, New York. He was upset that he could not attack New York City. The home of Wall Street. That would have been a great target and a great way to sacrifice himself. Instead, he was ordered to attack Albany. A city of only about 100,000 people. New York City could have 8 to 10 million people at any one time. Think of the panic. How many would be trampled in the confusion? A glorious vision. Instead, he had to attack a small city, 150 miles away from the biggest city in America. He would do his duty for the good of the cause. His only comfort was that he shared the same frustration with 31. Sacramento would not be as good a target as Los Angeles or San Francisco.

It was a hot, sunny day in Salt Lake City. #45 was walking east on South Temple Street. He was only a block away from his hotel. He thought he would go to the mall and have a look at his target. He turned right onto South Main Street. City Creek Center was just a block away. An easy walk. This mall had almost a hundred stores and restaurants. It would be crowded. It was always crowded, and that was great. More victims, more panic. In a city of infidels, his death would have great meaning. His death would accomplish much. He was so deep in thought that he did not see the dark grey car coming out of the parking garage. #45 was walking across the driveway when the car struck him. The impact knocked him down. People were screaming and running towards him. A man in some kind of uniform ran towards him. Was he police? No, he carried no weapon. He must be security. #45 could not let himself be detained. He started to stand up when several people grabbed his arms to help him stand up. The driver of the car jumped out of his vehicle and also tried to help. There were now three people holding him and a security guard rushing towards him. He kept saying that he was okay. People on the street were filming this with their accursed cell phones. Someone said they would call for the police and an ambulance. The situation was out of control. #45 fought to get away. The bystanders thought he was having some sort of medical episode. They held on to him, lest he fall and hurt himself. #45 demanded to be released. One woman heard him and let go. She did not want to be sued for trying to help. The other two men held on to him. He continued to struggle when he saw a black and white SUV pull up. It had lights flashing on its roof. #45 panicked. The one thing he was told never to do, he did. With his free hand, #45 pulled the grenade out of his pants pocket. He could not leave it in his room, lest it might be found. He held the grenade up high and screamed for people to leave me alone. The two men holding him released him and ran. The young Salt Lake City officer had only seen a grenade on TV and in the movies. He yelled at #45, "Drop the grenade." The streets were in full panic mode, everyone running but not sure where to go. #45 knew the police would arrest him and turn him over to the accursed CIA. He could not allow this to happen. They would torture him and make him talk. Better to die now. With his free hand, he reached for the ring at the end of the safety pin. #45 knew that once the pin was removed, all he had to do was release the grenade. The pin kept the "spoon" in place. With the pin removed and the spoon released, a spring under the spoon would send it flying. At the same instant, a striker would start the fuse. In 4 to 5 seconds, the grenade would detonate, hurling shrapnel in all directions. Once the spoon was released, there was no way to stop the explosion from happening. Officer Bradley Thompson had been a police officer for almost a year. He had graduated from the police academy and passed his field training evaluation. He had been on solo status for almost a month now. He never fired a weapon except at the police academy. Somehow, he was put on the day shift in a good neighborhood. His young wife was overjoyed. Her husband was safe and would be home at night.

#45 reached for the ring to pull the pin out. He never heard the shot. The supersonic bullet from Thompson's issued pistol hit #45 in the throat. The hydrostatic shock of the bullet ruptured a major artery and vein in #45's neck. His blood pressure dropped immediately, his hands dropped to his sides, and his vision went to grey and then black. #45 was dead before he hit the ground. The grenade was still in his hand. Thompson was frozen. He had not moved since the weapon fired. He had just killed a man. The shooting would be reviewed by Thompson's supervisor, internal affairs, the police chief, and the district attorney. All would say he did the right thing; he saved lives. The news media would make him into a hero. Thompson was sick to his stomach.

Detective James was the first detective on the scene. Thompson pointed at the grenade. James, at first, thought the rookie had panicked. He looked at the object in the dead man's hand. James has served in the Army and had thrown grenades during basic training and advanced individual training. This sure looked like a grenade. James called for the bomb squad and made a call to ATFE. The agent who answered the phone was very interested in a man with Middle Eastern features and a grenade. The detectives interviewed witnesses, collected evidence, and took measurements when a black Tahoe rolled up. "Here comes the feds," said James to himself. Two men in black suits and matching sunglasses exited the Tahoe. They approached James and flashed their credentials. "Do you have his identification?" asked the driver of the Tahoe, the older of the two agents. James showed them the dead man's passport, driver's license, and credit card. "Hand grenade?" asked the younger agent. "Hand grenade, M67," said James. The agents looked at each other and copied information from the documents James showed them. The older agent turned around quickly and walked away from James. The agent took out his phone and made a call.

Chapter Nineteen

The phone rang in the command post at Biggs Field. "Special Agent Hernandez," said the agent as he picked up the phone. "Sir, I am patching you into a call from agents in Atlanta." There was a click, and a voice came on the line. "This is FBI Special Agent Gavin. To whom am I speaking?" "This is FBI Special Agent Hernandez," Gavin said, "I was put through to you because you are working on some kind of terrorist plot." It was almost a question. Hernandez said, "Something like that, what do you have?" Gavin was not read into the program. "I am in Atlanta. Some guy was walking past a mall here. He was hit by a car. Looks like an accident. Well, when bystanders tried to help him, he pulled out a hand grenade. Bomb squad said it was real and live. He tried to pull the pin, and some local cop shot him. All his ID is fake, passport, driver's license, credit card, all of it." Hernandez waved wildly at the other agents to come closer. "Can we talk to him, question him?" "Sorry," said Gavin, "The cop was a good shot. "Email me a photocopy of all, and I mean all of his paperwork and anything in his pockets. I need a close-up of his face. Overnight, all of it was directly to me. Find out where he was staying and search the room. Do not wait on a warrant, just do it now." "You know I can't search a room without a warrant. It's a civil rights violation, and it also makes the evidence inadmissible," protested Gavin. Hernandez got upset but remembered that Gavin had no idea about the plot. "In less than 5 minutes, you will get a phone call from the Attorney General. He will order you to do what I asked. I cannot tell you why, but it is critical for you to do as I asked." Hernandez hung up and approached the AG, who was looking at a large map of the United States. "Sir, I think one of the terrorists was just killed by local police in Atlanta. I need you to call the FBI agent on the scene. I told him to find and search the individual's room without a warrant. He understandably doesn't want to." Hernandez gave the agent's name and phone number. The AG took out his cell phone and made a call. After less than a minute, the AG hung up. "He will do as you asked."

"Okay, people, listen up, yelled the AG. The room went silent. A man with a fake ID was just shot and killed outside the biggest mall in Atlanta. Her had two hand grenades on him. He tried to use one. No one was hurt except the terrorist. We have people on the scene, but they do not know the whole picture. I think we should assume that our information is correct. While it is not the 4th yet, it is close enough. This guy may have been doing a recon or just jumping the gun. Either way, it is time to ramp this up. I want all 50 pictures immediately sent to the governor of each state. The same to the police chief of each capital city. Let them know of the pending attack on the 4th. Let them know these guys have two hand grenades and are ready to die. Until this is over, and that means all 50 are accounted for, no one goes home or takes a break. We only have a day and a half. I do not want these bastards to succeed. Any problems with cooperation, bring them to me immediately."

The pictures of all 50 men were posted on the wall. A list of state capitols was also posted on the wall. Telephones were dialed, and an email was sent. The noise in the room, with everyone talking at the same time, was deafening. It took a while, but everyone was notified. At the same time, numerous phone calls and emails flooded the center. "Was the information any good? What is the source of the information? Is this a drill? You can't expect me to commit all these resources to a meeting to discuss the situation." The Attorney General was getting very upset.

"OK, everyone, listen up," he yelled over the sounds of dozens of people talking. "If you get any kind of pushback, call me on the phone immediately. Do not try to argue, let me do that." The AG realized what he had just signed up for. He needed another cup of coffee. The local colonel who greeted him when he arrived and helped to set up the command post had provided two coffee pots, donuts, and sandwiches, and made sure the restrooms were stocked with lots of bathroom tissue. The colonel knew the next few days would be insane.

"Sir, Mr. Attorney General," yelled a young DHS agent. As the AG approached the agent, the agent said, "Sir, I have the Governor of California on the line. He does not believe me or that the situation even exists. Says he never heard of it." The AG grabbed the phone out of the agent's hand. "Wakefield, this is the U.S. Attorney General. Don't talk, just listen. At one P.M. on the fourth, a terrorist will explode two hand grenades in the mall in Sacramento. We are not sure which mall it is. It might be the Westfield Galleria, due to its size, or the 500 Capitol Tower Mall, due to its location. It could be another mall; you have so many of them. Look at your news. What just happened in Atlanta? That is coming to you. The terrorist is there to die and to take as many Americans as he can. We sent you pictures of the terrorist, but we do not know which one is coming for you. Now, get your cops in and around those malls on the fourth. No uniforms, that might provoke him. There will also be federal agents, not sure yet which agency, at the malls. Wakefield, if you do not do everything in your power to stop this, the deaths of your citizens will be on your hands, and I will make sure the press knows who dropped the ball." The AG hung up without waiting for a response. Federal agencies were being tasked to have agents in every state at the malls. Investigators from state law enforcement were driving to their capitols to set up surveillance. City detectives were told to drop their cases and respond to the malls in their city. So ended July 2nd.

Chapter Twenty

The man in black sat at his desk in Shiraz, Iran. He was not really a "man in black," or was he? He always wore black suits, quality black suits, to work daily. His office overlooked the Nasir al Mulk Mosque. This beautiful building was over two hundred years old. Of all the mosques he had visited, this one held a special meaning to him. He visited it often. After all, he had the time. As the regional director of the Iranian Ministry of Intelligence and Security, no one questioned his comings and goings. His area of responsibility covered a huge area, all the way to Bandar Abbas. His real name was Arzhang Hosseini. At work, he was called "Sir" or "Director." He had worked his way through the Ministry by being totally loyal and totally ruthless. He was loyal to the State, and woe to anyone who was deemed less than loyal.

He had started in the Ministry as a young analyst fresh out of Al-Mustafa International University in Qom. This time at school helped him to make contacts who went to other parts of the world. It also made him deeply religious. The world-famous Fatima Masumeh Shrine gave him the belief that Islam was the only true faith. That all others must convert or be eliminated. This hardcore dedication pleased his superiors and helped to advance his career. His first field assignment was to recruit a German professor whom he had met through the University. The professor had many friends in the German military. He would be a good source of intelligence.

However, the recruitment did not go as planned. The professor realized that he was being recruited and left the meeting. The professor said he was going to report Arzhang to German intelligence so he would be known as a recruiter for Iranian intelligence. Arzhang strangled the professor with his hands. It wasn't that hard to do. His body disappeared into the desert. There was so much desert in the area. When he told his boss what had happened, he was afraid he would be terminated for not accomplishing the mission. Instead, he was promoted to full field agent status. This dedicated man could be of use to the State.

Now, as a regional director, he had heard of the sea battle and the hatred the son had for the Americans. Before he could recruit him, a mutual friend let Arzhang know about the burning vengeance that Mohammed held for the Americans. The plan Mohammed came up with was so simple and would be so effective. That Mohammed would use his own money to finance the operation. He would use his shipping contacts to get the men to Mexico and then to the States. He would pay for the transporting and lodging of the other men. There was only one thing wrong with the plan. Arzhang would take care of that shortcoming.

The idea of striking 50 state capitols at once was brilliant. Mass panic, economic disaster, a government in chaos. A wonderful plan. The only shortcoming was that Mohammad did not plan to strike the nation's capital, Washington, D.C. After all, it was not a state, but a district. Whatever that was. It was the hub of American politics. Striking there would magnify the effect of Mohammed's attack. It would take America years to recover. The Americans would hold hearing after hearing, trying to find someone to blame. Their ability to project power around the world would be at an end. The American military would be recalled from the Middle East to safeguard America.

The attack would occur on July 4th. Mohammed was right about the symbolism of attacking on that date. Mohammed was also right about all the attacks happening at the same time. This would cause mass confusion and panic. What time should the attack on D.C. occur, and what should be attacked?

Arzhang would personally supervise the attack on Washington, D.C. There was no reason Mohammed should get all the credit for the operation. He would find a few more volunteers to go to Washington. He could easily bring the grenades in. After all, one of his covers was as an economic attaché. That would give him diplomatic immunity, and his luggage was not subject to inspection. A half dozen hand grenades would fit in his luggage. At the end of this mission, he would probably be promoted. He would have accomplished what no one else could. The Ministry would promote him and move him to Tehran. Maybe as director of operations. That would come with a nice pay raise, a better home, and much more status. He thought for a while about the question of where and when. The time part would be easy. All attacks at the same time. Emergency responders would be running to all 50 sites. Communications systems overloaded. The American leadership in chaos. Yes, at the same time. Before people could take shelter, some would arm themselves. He did not want to face a group of angry armed citizens. The police could detain him, but that was all. He had diplomatic immunity. Armed citizens had no such restrictions. If he were found out, his life would be over.

Now he knew when. The next question was where? He considered some of the monuments. They always had crowds of people; they were lightly guarded, if guarded at all. Getting onto the White House grounds was possible. It had been done several times. Still, it was very heavily guarded, and his men would be immediately engaged by security forces. The Capitol building would be open. He could book a tour online and have his men circulate through the building. The explosives would kill many, but would do little damage other than to some painting on the walls. Real grenades are not like the ones he had seen in the movies. Movie grenades take out entire buildings. Real ones spray shrapnel in a five-meter circle. Lethal, sure, but the blast would not affect the structure of the building. The Pentagon was out of the question. It was heavily guarded by armed security. All backpacks were inspected. Just getting into the building would be extremely difficult. It was not a tourist attraction. He had to think about this a bit more. Visions of death, destruction, and promotions danced in his mind.

Chapter Twenty-One

By the morning of July 3rd, police detectives and state troopers were in their state capitol for a briefing. All were in civilian clothes and were told not to shave that day. They all wore loose-fitting clothing with their weapons hidden. This would be handguns only. You cannot walk around a mall with an assault rifle or shotgun hidden on your person and not go unnoticed. Besides, high powered bullet might go through the target and hit a bystander. Totally unacceptable. Each city had set up a command post in a law enforcement building. There, assignments would be given out, and briefings conducted. Each officer was emailed the photographs of the terrorists. Some of the pictures were grainy, but that would have to do. The officers could scroll through the pictures without drawing attention to help confirm an identity. Being on a phone in a mall was so commonplace that no one would pay any attention to it. After the briefing, the photographs of the terrorists were projected on a large screen. The picture stayed on for ten seconds. Then the next picture was shown. This was kept on a continuous loop. The pictures were shown over and over. Officers reviewed maps of the streets around the mall and the layout of the mall. They worked out who would be where. Still, the photos were projected on the screen.

At the same time, dozens of federal agents from various agencies were at the federal building in each capital. Many had traveled all night to be there. Time was the enemy right now. The U.S. Attorney for that area was the briefer. In a few states, the U.S. Attorney was not available, in which case, the chief deputy conducted the briefing. It was made clear to the agents that this was a very serious matter. Anyone not pulling his or her weight, anyone not being a team player, would be reassigned to counting seals in the Aleutian Islands. There was laughter throughout the room. The briefer told them that this was not a joke. The stability of the nation was at stake. The room quieted down. There were FBI agents, U.S. Marshals, Homeland Security Agents, Customs Agents, and a few Postal Inspectors. Agents from the Bureau of Alcohol, Tobacco, Firearms, and Explosives were also there. They could provide expertise for the safe handling of the grenades, once they were secured. They also provide a short tutorial about grenades, how they worked and how to stop them from going off. In Alaska and Hawaii, agents of the Coast Guard Criminal Investigative Service were also present. Every resource would be needed and used. By the end of the next day, the country would survive or not. This was no time for halfway measures.

The Attorney General was briefed on the massive effort being made. It was time to make a phone call. "Mr. President, if you have a few minutes, let me bring you up to date on what we know and what we have done so far."

The President listened without interrupting the AG. "Tom, you have done a great job with limited time and resources. I hope it is enough, "said the President.

"I will talk to the Director of National Intelligence as well as the Chairman of the Joint Chiefs about this. There is little they can do to help out right now. I was going to put all military bases on alert, but that might delay the attack. It is a holiday, and most of the troops are off. I did direct that all military hospitals stay fully staffed on the 4th, in case there are mass casualties and the civilian hospitals can't handle the load. The DNI better make every effort to find out who is behind this. They will be dealt with, and I mean dealt with."

"Thank you, Mr. President," said the AG. "Sir, I need to go. Tomorrow will be a very busy day. I will be at this number until this is over, whatever that means."

"Good luck, Tom, the nation is counting on you." The President hung up the phone and rubbed his head. He will not be going to sleep until this was over.

The President called the DNI. As the Director of National Intelligence, he oversaw eighteen national-level intelligence agencies. Most people could name a few, but rarely could anyone outside of the intelligence community name them all. He was a political appointment. The degree of intelligence background varied from one DNI to another. "Yes, Mr. President?" answered the DNI. "Harold, I do not care what it costs, or what methods you use, I want to know who is behind this upcoming attack. This must not go unanswered. I am calling the Chairman next. We will have a response to whoever planned this, and I do not care where they are hiding." "Yes, Sir. We have a few leads but nothing solid yet," said the DNI. "I want an update every three hours, progress or not," the President replied. He hung up the phone.

The next call went to the Chairman of the Joint Chiefs of Staff. Army General William "Bill" Harper. The four-star general graduated from ROTC and went into the infantry. He worked his way up by doing more than was expected. He graduated from Airborne school and was the honor graduate from Ranger school. He had never worked harder in his life. He has lost weight but learned that limits were usually in one's mind, not in one's body. After commanding a rifle company in the 82nd Airborne Division, he applied for and was accepted to Special Forces Training. His career was stellar. Various command and staff positions around the globe. He always volunteered for combat assignments. The true test of a military person. It also helped with career advancement. He had an assignment as an instructor at and later as the head of the Special Warfare Center. However, with more and more ranks, there wer less and less field assignments. The only combat in this assignment was with Congress. He had to explain why every dollar was needed for each project. The vast majority of Congress did not have military, let alone combat experience. "Sir," said his aide, "The President is calling, secure line." Harper picked up the phone and said, "General Harper here." The flat-toned voice replied, "Please hold for the President." The President never waited on the phone.

"Bill, I have another job for you." "Yes, Mr. President." "The DNI is working to find out who is behind all this." The Chairman fully knew what "all this" was all about. "I want your folks to make plans to remove the people who are behind this as soon as the DNI figures it out. I do not know where these people might be, so be ready for any place. I know that is asking a lot, but I want a quick response for the person or persons who organized this attack."

"Yes, Sir," said Harper. "One question, Mr. President. Is this a kill or capture mission?" He did not like asking this, but in this day and age, Harper had to protect himself and his forces. There was a slight pause, then,

"I don't care. Take them off the board. Get our troops home safe." The connection was broken. Harper looked up at the American Flag hanging in his office. Never a clear-cut answer. Harper would have to make a lot of phone calls quickly to get a meeting with all the Joint Chiefs. Within the hour, the five four-star officers sat around a table in a soundproof room. Harper briefed the others on what was known. He also briefed on what was being done. "I want all of you and your people to come up with a variety of OPLANS to engage a target on the land or sea. Near a coast or deep inland, on a variety of terrains. The Army Chief of Staff looked at the Chairman and said, "Bill, you know the 82nd Airborne has a company on ready alert and a battalion ready on short notice." "Yeah, Mike, it hasn't changed since I was a lieutenant." Admiral Stephens, the Chief of Naval Operations, asked, "You want an Operational Plan to cover anywhere in the world, and you want it now?" "Glad you got it." Harper smiled. "I know this seems impossible, but right now, a bunch of cops in 49 states are trying to stop a single person they have never met or seen. All they have is a grainy photograph. Crank up your Plans folks, and call JSOC and get their input." The Joint Special Operations Command was a primer counter terrorist organization. People from all services served in JSOC. The screening process to get in was harder than an applicant could imagine. Always ready for deployment, they were the best of the best and were so equipped with the best equipment. Most of their missions were never spoken about. The Commandant of the Marine Corps jumped in, "My Marines are ready now, Anytime, anyplace." "Now if we only knew the place," said the Chief of Staff of the Air Force. "I will get a few B-2s ready. Some with cruise missiles and others with guided munitions. Just say where." The meeting ended with a lot of head shaking. This was an operation they had never planned for with so little detail. The generals and admiral returned to their offices. Their staff would be shifting into overdrive within the next hour. No one would go home tonight. So many possibilities to plan for.

All the military staff were alerted. The different major commands were also alerted. It was thought that the area of operations was with Central Command. CENTCOM had the Middle East. But who could say? Maybe this threat came from Asia. The Pacific Command in Hawaii alerted every ship and Marine to "be ready."

Again, not sure for what, but ready for an instant deployment. Naval vessels received a full load of shells and missiles. Marines cleaned their weapons again. They were surgically clean. The Air Force had their long range bombers ready. The bombers at Whiteman Air Force Base were fueled. Cruise missiles and guided munitions were wheeled out and parked next to the aircraft. Armed Air Police stood watch over the planes and bombs. Trucks pulled up in front of the barracks of the 82nd Airborne at Fort Bragg, North Carolina. The alert company put their gear in the trucks and waited for the move-out order. At nearby Pope Air Force Base, C-17 cargo planes were fueled and parked ready for the paratroopers. Trucks with parachutes and reserve parachutes were parked next to the terminal. Each paratrooper would get a parachute and reserve. They would put them on in the terminal and walk to the rear ramp of the C-17. They would walk up the ramp and sit on what some consider the least comfortable seats ever put on an aircraft. Once inside, the plane could fly anywhere, with in-flight refueling, and drop the paratroopers wherever they needed to go.

The American military was ready to strike and strike hard at those who were planning to cripple America. Now they just need a target.

Their target, the mastermind of this plot, was sitting at home in an upscale home in Bandar Abbas. He looked at his watch and calculated the time in the United States. He knew each time zone. Sure, this cost him many millions of dollars, but he did not care. His father would be avenged. He had two televisions in his home. He had one in the bedroom and one in his living room. One would be set for the BBC and the other for Press TV. As soon as something happened, he would know and rejoice.

Chapter Twenty-Two

It was the third of July. While the President, his cabinet, and the military planned, local police departments in every city were also making plans. Could they be sure about which mall was going to be attacked? Of course not, so plans would have to be developed for other malls in the city. Numerous two-officer teams reviewed photographs of the terrorists. Not knowing which face to look for made this task exhausting. Entrances to the malls, as well as exits not usually open to the public, had to be covered. However, the coverage had to be discrete. The job was to see the terrorist before the terrorist saw the police. Standing at the door would not work. Officers reviewed the floor plan of each mall. There was no way to tell where or when the terrorist would enter the mall. The police only knew the time the grenades were to go off. The terrorist could enter the mall hours before, eat lunch, go shopping, and then kill as many Americans as he could.

Most of the officers were city police. However, many states provided state troopers to assist. They were paired with city police who knew the area better. They would spend the day walking around the mall. Trying to identify a face out of a pack of 49 pictures, before the face identified them and killed as many Americans as he could. There would also be a few unmarked cars circling the mall. No option was discounted.

Federal officers from various agencies also planned to walk the malls. All states have federal officers. Some have a lot more than others. States like New York and California had the most. Some states, like Wyoming and Montana, had far fewer. The majority of the federal agents were FBI. They were trained as investigators. Luckily, many of them had training as undercover agents using soft clothes or relaxed appearances. There were also agents from various other agencies. They would also walk the mall. There was who doubted they would be effective. However, every set of eyes would increase the chances of stopping the attack. Probably the best agency for tracking people was the U.S. Marshals. A very old organization that hunted wanted criminals on a day-to-day basis. Of course, they usually had a description of the wanted person. They would make do with just a photo.

While all this preparation was being made, Arzhang and two of his associates were landing at Reagan Airport in Washington, D.C. The American Airlines flight had left London Heathrow Airport and flew to John F Kennedy Airport, nonstop. After an hour and a half layover, they took off for DC. It was a very short flight. Arzhang's associates had never been outside of Iran. They looked out of the window almost the entire time. They had no idea of the green countryside of the East Coast of the United States. Arzhang had assured that his associates were given false identification, which showed they were part of the Iranian Mission. Therefore, they had diplomatic immunity and were not subject to search or detention. This allowed them to carry their grenades on their person, even on a commercial flight. Upon arrival at Reagan, their diplomatic passports allowed them to walk through customs without a word being said. They carried their carry-on luggage out the exit door. That was his only mistake. While the terrorists did not need luggage, they would be dead in less than 24 hours; carrying no luggage on an international flight might have drawn some attention. Arzhang had told the terrorists that he would go with them on their suicide mission. He lied. He would let them die and complete his mission. He would return home in triumph. The black Tahoe was waiting for them when they exited the terminal. The Tahoe was roomy and was one of the most common vehicles in Washington, D.C. No one would pay any attention to them. The vehicle exited the airport and headed north on Highway 1. The road turned into Highway 110, past Arlington Cemetery and the Marine Corps Memorial. The terrorist looked in awe at the sights. The vehicle turned right onto Constitution Avenue. Both the Lincoln Memorial and the Washington Monument were clearly visible. The vehicle turned north onto 23 Street NW. In just about a mile and a half, the Tahoe pulled into the Iranian Interest Section located at the Pakistani Embassy at 1250 23 Street NW. Iran did not have a formal embassy in the United States.

Once inside the Embassy, Arzhang met with the Iranian Ministry of Intelligence representative. He explained his mission and the terrorist plot. The representative was shocked and speechless.

"This is madness. It will bring the total wrath of the Americans down on our country; it will be the end," Arzhang smiled. "This operation has been approved at the highest level of our government. If you do not support the operation, you will be sent home as a traitor and in disgrace." The representative could not speak. He was stunned and in disbelief. He walked immediately to his office. Arzhang followed him. He picked up the secure phone and called Tehran. He would get to the bottom of this. After being transferred over and over again, the representative spoke directly to the Director of the Ministry. He started to complain about the operation when he froze. His mouth moved, but no sound came out. After about a minute, he hung up the phone and looked at Arzhang. "It will be as you wish," Arzhang smiled in triumph. "All I need is a place for my two friends and me to sleep tonight. In the morning, I will need transportation to my target. After that, you may do what you want to do."

Arzhang laid down in the bed. It was not comfortable, but it would do. He reviewed his plan in his head. The Americans would never expect it. The attack on the 50 malls would be devastating. His attack would kill so many more people. What made this attack his crown jewel was that it would be televised to the entire nation, live as it occurred. It would be televised, free of charge, by American television. He actually laughed out loud. Then he went to sleep.

Chapter Twenty-Three

It was early morning on the 4ᵗʰ of July. Many offices were closed. Banks and Post Offices were closed. Malls were open, boasting of holiday sales. It was the nation's birthday. Many people were going to go shopping for bargains or have fun with some sort of recreation. In Washington, D.C., traffic was lighter than normal except around the museums, monuments, and memorials. These areas were always crowded with tourists. The Smithsonian Museums were open. Over a dozen huge buildings containing treasures covering numerous topics, from art to history, to culture, to space. All free to enjoy. If that was not enough, the National Zoo was also free. In an expensive city, these were sights not to be missed. Arzhang awoke and looked at his watch. He had time. He dressed and went out for coffee. He relaxed and watched people going about their own business. People in their own little world. All that was about to change.

It was still dark in Alaska and Hawaii. #49 and #50 were asleep. It would be their last day of life. They would wake up in their hotel rooms and pray. They had done this every day of their adult life. They believed that even though suicide was forbidden in their Bible, blowing oneself up to further the Islamic cause was acceptable. Indeed, they expected a great reward when they got to Heaven. They would soon find out.

Across the continental United States, 48 terrorists, one in each capital city, was getting up and getting dressed. Some prayed, some did not. Some ate breakfast, some did not. In a little while, they would all head for the malls in their city. All made sure to check the time on their watches. They would detonate their explosives at exactly the right time. The West Coast of the United States would be struck at 5:00 P.M. This time was picked because of Arzhang's master plan. He wanted the East Coast attacked at 8 P.M. Not only would darkness add to the chaos, but the target he picked would be on American television. The entire world would see the power of his country.

On that morning, hundreds of law enforcement officers were getting ready for work. City, county, and state cops put on their body armor and uniforms. These were the cops on the beat. Next came the gun belts. Unlike TV cops, these belts were heavy. There was a pistol and holster, one or two sets of metal handcuffs, each in a case. They carried spare ammunition, a flashlight, chemical spray, a wooden or metal baton, and a Taser. There were also various keys for their vehicles, handcuffs, offices, and buildings. After all that, a few pens and a notebook hardly mattered. Federal officers and local officers assigned to the malls were not in uniform. They, of course, had their pistols and spare ammunition. A set of handcuffs tucked into their belts. They all carried cell phones. These would replace the obvious police radios, which were bulky. Their badges were hidden, but could quickly be displayed when necessary. These officers would arrive several hours ahead of the time the bombs were supposed to go off.

Everyone had a mission and a purpose, it seemed except Supervisory Deputy U.S. Marshal Mark Tower. A member of the oldest Federal Law Enforcement agency in America. The alerts had been nationwide. Every state capitol was on alert. Dozens of law enforcement officers were deployed to stop the threat, except Tower and his deputies. Tower was told that all 50 state capitols were covered. Lots of cops and feds. The nearest capitals to his location were Richmond, Virginia, and Baltimore, Maryland. They were covered. Something just didn't sit right with Tower. Was it that he was being left out of the most important manhunt in U.S. history? Well, yes, that was part of it. There was something else. He just could not figure out what was bugging him. Something was wrong. But what?

Tower had been with the Marshal's Service for fifteen years. He had served as an infantry company commander in the elite 82nd Airborne Division at Fort Bragg, North Carolina.

Tower called over to his senior deputy and good friend, James Jackson. Jackson had been a deputy for ten years. He had a bachelor's degree in criminal justice and was working on his law degree at George Washington University. Jackson had served in the Marine Corps and had one combat deployment. He made it home safely. He was the go-to guy when someone needed a warrant or a subpoena. He knew the law backwards and forwards. Tower had met Jackson at GWU. He was working on his Master's degree in Criminology. They made a great team. The Marshal's Service thought so also.

"Jim, what are we missing?" asked Tower. "I have read the intelligence reports over and over. We are missing something." Jackson did not know what they had missed, but he knew Tower's hunches deserved a second look.

"Okay, let's review. This Iranian lost his father when their cargo ship opened fire on the Navy. They were running weapons. This guy, Mohammed, somehow gets 50 suicide bombers together and gets them to Mexico. He arms them with hand grenades and somehow gets them to every state capitol in the U.S. The cartel makes a deal with the DOJ. This information and photos for the #2 most wanted person that we have in custody." "Right," said Jackson, nodding his head. "They have every available cop and fed all over the malls. They will try to identify and stop these terrorists before they can set the grenades off. We even have the time of the attacks." "And we just sit here," said Tower, shaking his head. "There is a piece missing," Tower stated. "This guy hates the US, but he does not have the resources to do this on his own. Intel reports say prior to this, he was an honest businessman and not some kind of religious fanatic. Where did he get 50 suicide bombers and 100 hand grenades? Why stop with state capitols with all these resources?"

They stared at each other. Then they realized what the missing piece was. A look of shock appeared on both their faces. "Whoever is supporting this plan is not going to stop with state capitols. He is going to hit the Capitol in D.C.," yelled Tower. At the same moment, Jackson had had the same thought. An attack on the D.C. area at the same time. But where?

"Okay, there are two parts to this problem: who and where? We know when, why, and how." Jackson agreed. "I'll take the who if you can guess where." Tower smiled. "I'd better be more than a guess. If I am right and we blow this, there will be city-wide panic and a lot of innocent people killed or injured. Jackson went back to his desk and got out his government phone book. There would be a lot of calls made and little time to do them. Tower got out a map of D.C. and posted it on the wall with tacks. He sat in his chair and stared at the map.

Jackson's first call was to the FBI. Even though the Bureau and the Marshals worked for the same boss, there had always been a communications problem. That was a polite way of saying information did not freely flow between the two agencies. The woman at the counter terrorism desk said she had nothing new since the AG called and briefed everyone. Jackson said thanks and called the Central Intelligence Agency. They were not a law enforcement agency and rarely shared intelligence with agencies outside of the Intelligence Community. After being transferred from one office to another, always verifying who he was and why he was calling, the answer came back with no new information. Everyone was focused on the threat to the remaining 49 states. He made more calls. To the Defense Intelligence Agency, the National Security Agency, DHS, and the DEA. All said the same thing, nothing unusual outside of the national alert that was in progress. Jackson was running out of ideas. He had a thought about terrorists coming into the country. Maybe some came legally? His next call was to the State Department. The State Department has its own Bureau of Intelligence. While not a huge organization, their worldwide contacts might have turned something up.

"U.S. Deputy Marshal Jackson here. I need to speak to someone about the possibility of a terrorist coming into the country legally." There was the usual transferring of the call. Finally, after several minutes of "elevator music," Jackson heard, "Department of State, Phillips here." Jackson explained the situation and his concern about another attack. There was a pause.

Phillips answered, "No one on the terrorist watch list has entered the country, at least not through a regular checkpoint or using their real name."

Jackson hung his head in failure. "Anything unusual at all in the last 48 hours?" There was a silent prayer in the question. "You know, now that you mention it, give me a second." Jackson held his breath. "I am not sure if this means anything, but a mid-level member of the Iranian Security Service landed at Reagan. This is not anything special. They come and go as they wish. They all have diplomatic immunity. What made it stand out was that he had two guys with him. Both had diplomatic passports, but their names were not on any of our lists." "You have lists of good guys and bad guys?" asked Jackson.

"Sure, we know everyone in their mission here. Also, these guys did not look the part. Can't say why, but they looked wrong. They did not do anything wrong, just that there was something about them. They exited the airport, got into a black Tahoe, and drove off."

Jackson was now excited. "Can you send me their pictures and anything else you have on them?" "Sure," said Phillips, what is going on?" "Just a feeling for right now, but we have to find them right now." "Probably at the Pakistani Embassy. Iran does not have an embassy here." "Thank you so much," said Jackson, and hung up the phone. Three new Iranians get here the day before the 4th. One of them is a midlevel intelligence officer. They usually never travel in a group, unless everyone in the groups was an operative. That was rare. Jackson thought about this for a few moments, then he noticed his computer screen. He had a new email from Phillips. Jackson opened the file. There were photos of the three Iranians and a short bio on the known operative. Jackson took this to Tower.

"Great work, Jim," beamed Tower. "See what the CIA has on this guy. We have a name and a face now. Probably no way to find him here in the district. We need to find the target." Jackson was back on the secure phone to the CIA. "He is a mid-level intelligence officer with the Iranian Ministry of Intelligence and Security. He is suspected in several assassinations, but no real proof. His career is going very well, and he may be ready for another promotion. Right now, he is a regional director."

"Which region?" asked Tower.

"He has everything from Shiraz to the Persian Gulf and down to Bandar Abbas."

"Isn't this Mohammed guy who is running this attack from there?" asked Tower.

"Sure is, and Mohammad has a lot of political connections in the area. It would not surprise me if he found this guy or he found Mohammed."

Tower asked, "Will the CIA help us in this manhunt?"

"No, their official answer is that they are forbidden to operate on US soil."

Tower responded, "Not like that has ever stopped them before. What is the real reason?"

Jackson shook his head, "It doesn't fit into their concept of what is happening here today. They believe the AG that there will only be 50 terrorists hitting 50 capitols. They don't think there will be more. Besides, the leader of this mess is supposed to be Mohammed, who is back in Iran now. CIA says they will watch him. After this is over, there will probably be some action against him." Said Jackson.

"Okay," said Tower. "Get the rest of the team in here now. Some may be home, I don't care. We need to figure out what the target is. 8 P.M. will get here faster than we want. We have to identify the target, get to it, and stop the attack. Did you have anything better to do today?" smiled Tower. "Well, I was going to watch the fireworks with the family." Let's hope the scheduled kind are the only ones fired tonight." Jackson started making calls to the other team members, telling them to get to the office now! Tower was using stick pins to hang maps of Washington, D.C. up on every wall. The target had to be identified quickly so they could get into position to stop three terrorists somewhere in the District from attacking the fabric of America.

Chapter Twenty-Four

Within an hour, the other four members of the team were in the office. Most had stayed close to the office. They knew about the planned attack and were all disappointed when the team was told to stand down. They all lived close to the Marshal's office at 1215 South Clark Street in Alexandria, Virginia. Just west of Reagan Airport and south of Highway 395, traffic was still terrible, especially when one was in a rush. They knew they would not be called in on a legal holiday without a new case or a good reason. Cops needed family time, also.

As soon as all the deputies were there, Tower stood and addressed them. "We all know that 50 terrorists entered this country illegally from Mexico. That each one is armed with two US-style hand grenades. Each was to go to a state capitol, find the biggest mall, and kill as many civilians as possible before the terrorists killed themselves. I know we are all upset about not being used to hunting these terrorists down. We are still the best manhunters out there." Tower paused and looked at his team. There were a lot of nodding heads in agreement. "Jim and I have come up with something interesting. It is our thought that there will be a 51st attack on the nation's capital." The room got instantly quiet. "We have learned that an Iranian intelligence officer and 2 other men came to DC yesterday and have disappeared. We have checked with everyone, and no one has seen them. We are guessing that they are in the Pakistani Embassy. I need two things right now. I need someone to go to the embassy, park outside, and watch for these three people. We have current photos of each from when they arrived in DC. The rest of you, we need to brainstorm what their target is. We have zero intel on what it might be, other than some place to kill lots of civilians and probably make this attack the biggest of them all. The 50 men are just suicide bombers. The guy running this op is a trained professional. This is his big score."

U.S. Deputy Marshal George Samuels said, I'll go." He grabbed his "street bag" and headed to the parking lot. The bag contained food, water, binoculars, a spare baseball hat, a phone charger, and spare ammunition. He got into an unmarked car and headed for the embassy area. This was not a 4 door Ford or Chevy SUV; it was an old Pontiac. It had dents in it and faded paint. It did not look like a police vehicle. The only problem was that after sitting for hours in the same spot, someone might call in a suspicious vehicle call to the local police. He did not want to flash his badge to them and give away his cover.

The rest of the team gathered around Tower and Jackson. "We think this spook and his two buddies will attack at 2000 hours today. Everyone get to a map, work in teams, and get me a best guess on where they will strike. You have 20 minutes, and then we will get together and brainstorm this. Wherever it is, we have to be there long before 2000 hours. Evans, you work with Jackson." Tower stared at his map of the District.

Twenty minutes later, they all stood before Tower. Jackson started. "At first, we thought they would attack a monument or museum. Lots of tourists. Then we realized that the Smithsonian Museums and the National Zoo close long before 8, so not civilian casualties. The same is true of the Washington Monument. The Capitol building would also be closed. Now, the Lincoln and Jefferson Memorials are open. There is a park ranger at each until 2200 hours. Still, the ranger would not be able to stop three terrorists. Probably not a lot of tourists there at that time of night. They would kill some, but hardly enough to make the kind of statement they want to make."

The other team joined in. "There are several malls in the DC area, but nothing to make an attack there stand out. There are numerous official buildings, but they will be closed for the holiday. We considered that they would attack Arlington Cemetery. At that time of night, there would be few people there. A grenade could blow up a headstone or grave marker, but that's about all. Even if they blew up President Kennedy's site, there would be no death or injury, the marker would be rebuilt immediately, and I think they would lose face for destroying a gravesite. Not very brave." The room went silent. Tower stared at the map. There had to be something he was missing.

He got a sick feeling in his stomach. His mouth went dry. "Oh God No," he yelled. The others looked at him, not knowing what was going on. "They are going to hit the Capitol Fourth celebration on the west lawn of the Capitol. There will be hundreds of thousands of people packed in the area. There will also be live national TV coverage of the events. The cameras will film the carnage and panic. It will be instantly televised across the country. All states and the federal capital hit at once. Live coverage showing the death, people stampeding over others, the authorities unable to stop thousands of people fleeing in terror." The room went silent again.

"Get on the phone to every law enforcement agency in the area. I know that is a lot, but we are going to need help on this. Get their email or fax and send them a copy of the pictures we have. The Capitol Police and the Park Police should be called first. The FBI and DHS next. Don't forget the DC Metropolitan Police. Make sure they know these are suicide bombers. Those de-escalation classes will not work here, and neither will the Miranda warning.

Deputies got on the phone and started dialing. There were a lot of loud voices. The room sounded like a convention. Tower called Samuels to see if there was any progress. There wasn't. Few people park on Embassy Row for hours; his cover might have been blown. After about 25 minutes, the team assembled. "DHS said they would send some agents to help. The FBI said they could not move agents around on a hunch. They said to call back if there was real proof." Said one of the deputies. "Son of a bitch," said Tower. "By that time, it would be too late." Another deputy advised that the Park Police, the Capitol Police, and the Metro cops would send plainclothes officers to walk among the crowd. "Okay," said Tower, "We will leave in about two hours. Until then, get your gear together and try to get some rest. It may be a very long night.

Chapter Twenty-Five

It was almost time for the attacks to begin. All the players were moving into position. The remaining 49 terrorists had made peace with themselves and their deaths. They were either all in the malls by now or approaching the malls. Many of them marveled at the luxury of the American people. Their stores had so much to sell. Food stores had a variety and quantity that they could not imagine. The people walked around, seeming to be having a good time. These were the enemy of Iran? What had they done to deserve this? They saw people walking around clearly and freely showing emblems of their faith. Most wore crosses, but some wore the Star of David. Were these people Israelis? No, they were Americans, but they must support Israel. Israel was the enemy of Iran. That is what they were told. They must complete their mission. They were told this was important.

The US Attorney General was still in the command center at Biggs Field. He had not slept in several days, and it was getting the better of him. He had coordinated with every agency he could. He had to call the White House every three hours, so any rest was hard to come by. He had made it clear to everyone that any agency that did not do 110% effort would need a new director within a week. There are no days off or vacations. Anyone with a badge would be working today. He was not aware of the ideas of the US Marshals in DC. None of the agencies that were contacted bothered to pass the information up the chain of command. There was no real evidence, only a hunch of a low-ranking supervisory Marshal. No ne else had seen this threat.

The President of the United States was in his operations center below the White House. From here, he could reach out and talk to anyone, just about anywhere. His staff had electronic maps up on screens. Every attack, if it occurred, would be color-coded. Green for the capture or death of a terrorist. Yellow for the capture or death of a terrorist and the death of 5 or less Americans. Red for the death of more than 5 Americans, and the terrorist not in custody. If red, the terrorist would have killed himself. Hospitals in all state capitols were put on alert for a mass casualty event. The President was ready to mobilize the National Guard, if needed. Military bases were put on alert. Military hospitals may be needed to handle casualties if local hospitals could not. Military aviation units and transportation units were ready to assist in the moving of casualties to hospitals. He wondered what else he could have done. He did not know. Someone else would probably second-guess him tomorrow.

Every cop in the capital cities was on duty. Many not in uniform. Walking in pairs around and in the malls. The same was true for numerous federal agents. On short notice, they had flown or driven to the capital cities. Each governor had set up a command center. From here, assignments had been given out. Plans for evacuation routes were assigned to the city police. In the event of an explosion, there had to be a clear path to hospitals. Every firefighter and paramedic was sitting in their vehicles, ready to respond on a moment's notice. They hoped the local cops would clear a path for them to the scene of the horror.

Mohammed looked at his Rolex. It was almost time. Less than an hour to go. The great United States would be attacked and crippled by his plan, his doing. His father would be avenged. Mohammad cared about little else. He had not gone to work in weeks. The business could run itself. Most thought he was still in shock over the loss of his father. He would sit in his home and watch the destruction on television. If he had not been a devote Muslim, he would be having a drink right now.

Arzhang and his two bombers had left the Embassy through a back exit. He had been informed that a car had been parked down the street from the Embassy for hours. There was a man seated in the car. He just sat there. There could be no way for the American police to know about him or his plot. He told no one. Nothing had been written down. Nothing had been said over the phone or the internet. This was a secure operation. Still, it did not pay to take a chance. This operation would go down in history, and he would rise to new levels of power and glory at home.

The Chairman of the Joint Chiefs was in a secure video conference with the Service Chiefs and the commanders of the major combat commands. He had asked them for their input as to what response should be given if and when this attack occurred. His chief intelligence officer reminded him that this attack was the work of one man and was not state-sponsored or sanctioned to the best of their knowledge. There were still questions as to how the terrorists were recruited and who provided the grenades. Until those questions were answered, striking the Iranian government or its military might be the wrong choice. An admiral sitting on his ship in the Gulf region insisted that the operation had to be state-sanctioned. His ships could send a hundred cruise missiles into Iran and knock out their power, communications, most military bases, and government offices. This without any risk to Americans. The Air Force general said his B-2 bombers could drop the "bunker-busting" bombs anywhere in Iran and destroy or at least cripple any underground facility. And so, the conversation went on. The Marines could make an amphibious landing in Bandar Abbas. Army paratroopers could jump in and secure the airport for the landing of heavier equipment or troops. Rangers could jump in and strike directly at the home of this Mohammad. Being the chairman was a great job. Sorting out all these options, the equipment and supplies necessary to complete the mission, its political aspect, and the chances of failure, or American losses, was not. He needed to decide and brief the President.

Chapter Twenty-Six

And so, it begins.

It was less than an hour before the attack was due to start. #50 was walking nervously into the mall in Honolulu. The area was full of people. Many looked like they were of Chinese, Japanese, or some other Asian descent. These were not the Americans #50 pictured. Wasn't Iran friendly with China? Would killing these Chinese cause problems for his country? He could not think of such things. His mission was to enter the mall, kill as many Americans as he could, and then die a glorious death. He would complete his mission. He had a grenade in each front pants pocket. The loose-fitting cargo pants he was given made carrying the grenades easy. He had a hand inside his pocket on the grenade. Just walk in, find a crowd, and death to the Americans. He was walking up the steps to the mall when something slammed into him. He was knocked to the ground with a huge weight on him. His chest slammed into the pavement. He saw stars and tried to see what was going on. A huge Hawaiian man had him pinned to the ground. His massive arms encircled him. He could not pull his hands out of his pockets. "Police, freeze!" yelled the big man into his face. If he could pull the pins out, at least he would take this man with him. Paradise called. The call did not go through. Another man grabbed his hand and kept them from moving. #50 tried to use his fingers to pull the pins from the grenades. Now the insult went further. A female, a female dared to grab his hands also. Did she not know her place? As if to answer the unspoken question, she pulled out a knife. #50 thought he would be knifed to death by a female. It was worse than that. The female used her knife to cut open his pants pockets. The blade cut him several times. Painful but not dangerous. With the pockets cut away, she removed the grenades from what was left of his pockets. Once this was done, the men handcuffed him and forced him to his feet. He was taken to a waiting police car and almost thrown into the back seat. The photos sent by the team in El Paso had provided the officers with what they needed. The officers could report that Hawaii was safe. The Honolulu police officers would turn their prisoner over to the FBI. They would make the announcement of the arrest. At least they would have to do the paperwork.

A few minutes later, #49 was standing in the middle of a huge shopping area in Juneau, Alaska. He was looking around, seeing all the people moving about. It was a holiday, and Americans spent money on holidays. What he did not see was the tall man standing near the sweatshirts for sale. He was clean-shaven and kept his hair very closely cut. He might have been a soldier. He was once, but not anymore. After his tour of duty at Fort Wainwright, he left the Army and applied to be an Alaska State Trooper. He had spent many months in the Trooper Academy in Sitka. There, Thomas Kinner became Trooper Kinner. The Academy was hard, in many ways, harder than Army basic training. In basic training, he learned the fundamentals and how to follow orders. As a Trooper, he had to know everything about everything and be able to work on his own. He learned the law, procedure, first aid, hand-to-hand combat, shooting his pistol, rifle, and shotgun. The standards were high. They had to be. A Trooper could be covering hundreds of square miles by himself. He was the beat cop, the community relations officer, and the detective. Yes, the training was intense. After graduating from the Academy, he was posted to the Anchorage area. There he rode for months with an experience officer who taught him how to apply the book work to real life. He was then allowed to operate on his own. He enjoyed the work and the scenery. Alaska was breathing. After a few years in Anchorage, he was transferred to the state capitol in Juneau. A nice town, with lots to see and do. Kinner's only problem was that Juneau was on an island. OK, a very big island, over 3,000 square miles. Still, the hunting and fishing were among the best in the world.

#49 did not like Juneau. Even in July, it was cool. Worse, it rained all the time. Two days out of every three. #49 loved the desert, not rain so much. This was a city of only 30,000 people or so. He has hoped for a bigger city to do more damage. Still, the results would be the same. Death and panic to Americans, and his heavenly reward for being a mass murderer. He looked around and saw about 50 people standing in a group near a food shop. They must have come off one of the numerous touring ships that dock here daily. "Good," he thought. Not only killing Americans, but also people from all over the country at the same time. Maybe this would hurt the tourism and cruise businesses also. It would be a good target. He was ready to die.

#49 took the first grenade out of his pocket. He held it high over his head and reached for the pin. This foolish technique, which he learned from movies, was his undoing. As he reached, he heard someone yelling. He didn't understand it, but it was too late now. The tourist heard the same yell, "State Trooper, drop it!" As #49 was about to pull the pin, Kinner fired his Glock pistol. He fired three times. All 3 bullets slammed into #49's chest. He was dead before he hit the ground. Kinner looked around to see if anyone else was hurt. All he saw were dozens of tourists filming the action with their cell phones. Kinner picked up the grenade and made sure the pin was properly seated. It was the first time he had shot someone. He did not like the feeling, no matter how necessary it was. Kinner called for his sergeant on his cell phone. He stood by the body until other troopers arrived to document the incident. Numerous photos would be taken. The tourists would be encouraged to submit a copy of their pictures for the investigation. Kinner knew there would be a long, detailed investigation of the shooting, no matter how obvious the situation was. He knew that this was a necessary requirement. He leaned against the wall and waited for the others to arrive.

Chapter Twenty-Seven

As the reports came in to the Biggs Field operations center, the colors on the electronic maps started to turn colors. There were a few green states. Most were yellow, and a few were red. The AG was upset. He knew finding one person in a crowded mall was very difficult, but there should have been less red on the map. "I want a short summary of what happened in each state. Nothing fancy, just a few lines." The heads of several analyses nodded quickly.

The AG got on the secure line to the President. "Mr. President, we are getting reports from all over the country. The attack we suspected has come to pass. I am guessing you will see this on your television momentarily. The news media will have a field day figuring out which story will come first. You know their motto, "If it bleeds, it leads." I think if there is any video, it will be shown first." The President was visibly shaken. "Tom, keep this line open. I want reports as they come in. I will have a staffer on the line if I have to step away." "Yes, Sir, Mr. President. At least we stopped most of them and greatly reduced the casualty numbers." "You did a good job, keep it up. The president handed the phone to a staffer, who listened patiently for any new information. Pen and pad at the ready. It would be a long night.

The calls from law enforcement all over the country started coming in. Slowly at first, and then a nonstop ring of phones. Stories of heroism and chaos, death and destruction. In Montgomery, Alabama, two citizens jumped on the terrorist and held him until the police arrived. Apparently, the terrorist needed some medical care, according to police. Body cameras showed the man injured before the police got there. In Tallassee, Florida, the terrorist displayed the grenade, yelled something, and was promptly shot by three shoppers. Unfortunately, in Sacramento, California, the terrorist threw a grenade from an upper level of the mall into a crowd that was on a lower level. He then ran into a crowded store, killing himself and 11 people in the store. Nine more were killed on the lower level when the grenade detonated above a crowd of shoppers. Shrapnel rained down on the innocent. Calls like this came in for the next hour or so. Emergency plans were activated in every state. Due to the localized death and destruction, the National Guard was not called in, but did remain on ready alert. There were tales of heroism. In Des Moines, Iowa, a farmer shopping with his family saw a terrorist pulling the pin out of the grenade. He ran and tackled the man. They both went through a plate-glass window. The farmer refused to release his grip on the grenade. To do so would have detonated the grenade in 4 to 5 seconds. When the police arrived a few minutes later. The farmer was on top of the terrorist, pinning him to the ground. The farmer still had a grip on the grenade. Police used a paper clip to secure the spoon or handle of the grenade. Once this was done, the farmer stood, and the police took the terrorist away. It seemed every person in the mall applauded as the farmer continued his shopping with his family. There was an event that went easier. In Bismarck, North Dakota, a terrorist pulled the pin and threw the grenade into a busy store. He waited; nothing happened. He waited a bit more, but nothing happened. The grenade was a dud. It would not explode. Several citizens saw this and stared at the terrorist. The terrorist started to cry. He had failed. He would not go to paradise. He forgot he had another grenade. He could have ended it. The police were there in seconds. More calls came into the operations center; the death toll nationwide was in the hundreds, and the injured totaled much more. It could have been so much worse if not for the actions of police, federal agents, and numerous brave citizens.

About an hour early, Tower and his team drove to the Capitol grounds as fast as possible. Deputy Samuels joined them. His stakeout was a bust. Now the six Deputy Marshals fanned out to try and find the three terrorists in a sea of patriotic Americans. The crowd was mind-boggling. There must be well over 100,000 people there, and the crowd was growing. How was it even possible to stop this attack? Tower and his men looked at the sea of people.

"Boss, how do we do this? asked Jackson. Tower just stared out and thought. "There are several entry points to the show. Those points have Park Police controlling them. They have the pictures of our terrorists. These guys will try to get in, away from these guarded checkpoints. There are numerous guarded entry points. Some are from Constitution Avenue; others are from 14th and 15th Street. Jim, if you wanted to sneak in and were motivated, how would you do it?" Jackson was hoping that his guess would not be the key to stopping the terrorists. "Well, it is getting dark, and I would come in by a place which is closed to visitors. I would come from either Northwest or Southwest Drive. I would find or make a gap in the fence. Come in slowly, between police patrols, and mingle with the crowd. There are no checkpoints there, and the Park Police are spread out kind of thin there." Tower nodded in agreement. "We have to trust the Park Police and the Metropolitan Police will keep the numerous checkpoints secure. If I flew halfway around the world for my crowning glory moment of my career, I would not try to just walk in." "How do we know which way they are coming?" asked one of the deputies. "We do not know," said Tower. "There are six of us and two possible paths. We go in teams of three. After all, there are three of them. We know two of them are suicide bombers; the third, this spy master, does not want to die. He wants to go home for a parade and promotion."

Tower looked at Jackson. "Take Wilson and Murray, I'll take Samuels and Carpenter. We will take the south side; you take the north. Be careful, these guys have nothing to lose." "Okay, boss, and let's all watch for citizens in the line of fire. No sense killing our own citizens with a stray bullet.

Arzhang and the two terrorists drove to the Capitol. They traveled east on Independence Ave. When they got to the Botanic Gardens, they pulled over and parked illegally on the street. The car was a rental, and they couldn't care less. The two terrorists thought they would all be dead within the hour. They walked north on First Street and then east along Southwest Drive. It was dark already. The sun had not fully set, but the heavy cloudy cover made it seem dark. The three men all wore dark clothing. The better not to be seen before they wanted to be seen. The men walked quickly and quietly through the grassy area. There were numerous barriers to prevent exactly what they wanted to do. The barriers were for the honest people, not for them. They observed numerous uniformed men and women walking the fence line. They all carried sidearms. Some carried long guns. Arzhang did not want to get into a shooting match with the police. That would ruin his televised attack. It would also minimize the number of deaths.

Arzhang finally found a break in the barriers. It was not much, but it was enough. They waited in the dark until the police patrols had passed. The three men quickly got past the barrier once there was a short break in the police patrols. They only had a few seconds, but they made it. Once they were well past the perimeter, they stood relaxed and walked towards the massive crowd. The two terrorists held their grenades in their pockets. They dreamed of paradise and knew it was only a few minutes away. Arzhang has to repeatedly tell them to act relaxed and not draw attention to themselves. No one else walked around with their hands in their pockets. Of course, having a hand grenade in each front pocket of their cargo pants, in the dark, should not draw anyone's attention. Arzhang would place each of the two terrorists apart from each other for maximum damage. Of course, he would stand away from them. He would tell them it was for the highest body count. In reality, he wanted to see his victory, but not so close as to sustain injuries.

Tower, Samuels, and Carpenter were spread out, moving slowly through the crowd. They were too far apart to talk or even yell. The music coming from the stage and the numerous speakers would be overpowering. The crowd was singing along also. Communications were impossible. However, the Marshals had practiced for such a situation. While they walked amongst the crowd, they constantly made eye contact. Head nods communicated which direction to walk or look. Jackson's group was doing the same on the north side of the crowd. They had no possibility of talking to each other either. Now it was walk, look, and pray.

Arzhang positioned the first terrorist. He was standing between two families. There was a total of five children within a yard of the terrorist. He looked around him and saw many other families, some people wearing shirts with the words "Army" or "U.S. Marines" on them. He could kill veterans of the American military. This made dying sweeter. As Arzhang was positioning the second terrorist, he saw a man who drew his attention. There was nothing obvious about the man. He was dressed in jeans, a t-shirt, and a loose dress shirt that was out of his pants and unbuttoned. He was looking around as if he had lost his family in the crowd. No, he was looking around like a predator; he was hunting something or someone. Arzhang knew, he knew, this man was hunting him. Arzhang had no idea how anyone even knew he was there, let alone his mission. He knew, he knew, this man was here for him. He also knew this man was not alone. He kept looking at other men, who were also looking around. Somehow, he had been discovered. He still had a way to win. Arzhang would order the two terrorists to use their grenades. In the panic and confusion, he would get away. If he could get back to the Pakistani embassy, they could get him out of the country. His diplomatic passport would protect him from the police. He did not want to be detained, as this would tarnish the glory of his plan. No, he could still go home as a hero.

The three men were starting to move in different directions when Tower signaled to Samuels and Carpenter. All three Marshals pushed their way through the crowd while never taking their eyes off the three men. The terrorist closest to Samuels pulled the grenade out of his pants pocket. He held it high over his head and started to pull the pin out. If he had held the grenade at chest height, the pin would have come out smoother. Again, too many movies. Samuels draws his Glock pistol from the holster on his hip. Before the pin could be pulled, Samuels shot the terrorist in the forehead. The bullet shattered the skull. The bullet and bone fragments shredded the brain. The terrorist dropped to the ground. Samuels raced to the body and secured the grenade. This was not like training. Shooting a real person in the midst of a crowd of innocent people is nothing anyone can truly prepare for. Samuels realized after he picked up the grenade that he was not breathing. He forced himself to breath and sat down next to the body.

The second terrorist was surprised by all this. He was told he would just kill himself and others and go to paradise. There was nothing about Americans shooting at him. He did not mind dying, but not until he completed his mission. There were dozens of people screaming and running in all directions. The single gunshot was enough to cause this. He pulled the grenade out of his pocket, and unlike the other terrorist, he held the grenade close to his chest. As he looked up to see where he would throw it to do the most damage, he saw a man charging at him. The man was focused on him, some type of police or military, thought the terrorist. Well, he was too late. He pulled the pin out. The terrorist screamed, "Infidel, I kill you." Carpenter was just a second or two too late to stop the pin from being pulled. The crowd was just too much for him to chance taking a shot. He dared not hit some civilian. Carpenter saw the terrorist standing in the middle of several families. It would be too difficult to run away. The terrorist was going to die right there and take a few families with him. He let out a curse under his breath. He knew what he had to do. He thought of his wife and son, whom he would never see again. Carpenter tackled the man, and they both went to the ground. Carpenter was on top of the terrorist. The grenade was under the terrorist's body, pressed up against his chest. Carpenter's body kept the terrorist pinned to the ground. Carpenter was saying a silent prayer when the grenade went off. He was lifted into the air. His chest was on fire. The pain was unbearable. His sight was blurring, and his field of vision was narrowing quickly. He told his wife and son that he loved them, and then everything went black.

Tower saw the explosion and cursed out loud. Carpenter was a good man, a loving husband and father. He was ready to give his life to protect others. Tower remembered something about "greater love hath no man… "Tower snapped back to reality. The third man, the leader of this attack, was backing away as quickly as he could. The chaos and panic prevented him from running away; the sea of people was moving all around him. Tower approached the man, gun drawn. While he knew that someone named Mohammad, who was halfway around the world, started this attack, the man in front of him was here, now, and trying to kill Americans. Carpenter, if still alive, was lying there because of this man. Arzhang knew he could not escape this man. He had a fire in his eyes. Maybe he could salvage something from this. He had no idea how many of the nationwide attacks had succeeded. If the Americans knew about him, did they know about the others? How? It did not matter right now. That would be learned later. Right now, he needed to live. He reached into his jacket pocket for his diplomatic passport. That would protect him from arrest. All they could do was deport him. Tower was within feet of Arzhang when he quickly reached into his jacket pocket. Tower took no chances and fired directly into the man's chest. Arzhang, with a look of surprise, dropped to his knees and then fell on his face. He was dead. Tower reached into the jacket pocket to secure the weapon. He came out with a diplomatic passport with a bullet hole in it. Tower could live with that.

By this time, there were dozens, if not hundreds, of police, firefighters, and emergency medical personnel there. The concert had stopped, and people were being told to stay where they were. Being run over by a crowd can kill you as dead as a bullet. Carpenter was evacuated to a nearby hospital. The paramedics who treated him hung and shook their heads. They would try, but he took part of the blast and a lot of shrapnel. Tower looked at his watch. It was 8:10 P.M. It had been a long day. He and Samuels would go back to their car and drive to the hospital to see if Carpenter survived. Jackson and his team would go to Carpenter's home and bring his wife and son to the hospital.

The attack on America was over for now.

Chapter Twenty-Eight

The Attorney General took a breath. He now had a report from all 50 states and, most surprisingly, from the District of Columbia. The information provided by the drug lord only spoke of the 50-state attack. The short report from the U.S. Marshals in D.C. made it seem as if the attack there came from this Iranian intelligence officer. They could not be sure. Since the U.S. and the Iranians had no political connection, it was hard to ask. The Secretary of State would go through a friendly country that had relations with Iran. Of course, Iran would deny the attack, and there was little proof. Their officer obviously went mad and then rogue. Again, a good story, with no proof.

The AG called the president with the final tally of death and destruction. "I guess it could have been much worse," said the president. "Yes, sir, without the information we got from the drug lord, casualties would have been several times worse. I want to let you know that the attack in D.C. was not on our radar. A Marshal figured it out, found the terrorists on the west side of the Capitol, and stopped the attack. One marshal is fighting for his life. He jumped on the terrorist and the grenade to shield the crowds."

The President thought and said, "I want to meet the Marshal who figured this out. I also want to visit the injured Marshal in the hospital. Does his family need anything?"

"I do not know Mr. President; it has been a bit busy here. I will have a final report to you within 48 hours."

"Make it 24 hours, I have to decide what our reaction to this is. We have dead in most states. Wounded are in hospitals all over the country. This is horrible and will not be tolerated. I want you to send a letter of commendation to the officers who stopped an attack in their state. I will take care of the Marshals who saved the Capitol Fourth celebration. The cameras there did not get to film the planned mass carnage. The country should be grateful for this."

The planning meeting consisted of the Joint Chiefs, the Central Command [CENTCOM] commander, representative from the CIA, DIA, and NSA. They had worked out several possible operations to respond to the attacks. There was no discussion about the use of nuclear weapons. Options ranged from attacks by strategic bombers to a cruise missile attack by naval surface or subsurface vessels. The insertion of paratroopers or Marines was given a low priority. Friendly death or wounded forces were not wanted. Besides, while it was easy to get them in, getting them out would pose several problems. Extraction by ship or aircraft for such a large force was not practical. The use of special operations forces was high on the list of options. The use of bombs or missiles could not ensure that Mohammad would be killed. Eyes on the target were desired. The choice was up to the President.

Mohammad was at home, watching television. He expected to see dead bodies and mass carnage throughout the United States. Instead, he watched reports of only a small number of dead in several states. There were lots of dead terrorists. He did not care about them. They meant nothing to him. Tools for his purpose. There was a report that did surprise him. Apparently, there was an attack by three Iranians in Washington, D.C. All three were killed, and only one police officer was severely injured. They showed a picture of one of the terrorists, it was Arzhang. He cursed out loud. Mohammad was livid. His plan had been hijacked, and it failed. How did the Americans know he was coming? He told no one. Unless the Mexicans told on him. That must have been it. He had been so careful. Now the mission had failed, and he did not have satisfaction. He would come up with another plan. He would only tell those he personally trusted. America must pay. But how?

The President was in the back seat of "The Beast," his heavily armor limo. When he travelled around the country or the world, the car was flown by the Air Force. It was bulletproof, could take hits from some heavy weapons, and had an air filtration system in case of chemical or bacteriological attack. It weighed many times that of a normal limo. He was going to Walter Reed Hospital. He was going to check in on the injured Marshal. While en route, he called the Chairman of the Joint Chiefs on the secure line. It was answered on the first ring. "Bill, this is the President. What do you have for me?"

"Mr. President, as of right now, our first choice is to insert a special ops team, make sure of the target, and then either kill or capture. Second choice is a cruise missile attack by the Navy. More destruction, no chance of friendly killed, injured, or captured. But we might not be 100% sure we got the target."

"Bill, I want you to full work up both plans. I will get with Langley and make sure the bad guy is at home when we come calling."

"Yes, Mr. President," the Chairman said.

The President broke the connection. He then called the Director of the Central Intelligence Agency. "I want every piece of information you can get on this guy. What is his favorite breakfast cereal? What TV shows does he watch? Most importantly, I want to know where he is every second of the day. His home layout and security go without saying. I want all this yesterday. I am not going to sit back and let him get away with this. I will clear this with the DNI. Use any national assets you need." The President hung up the phone as they arrived at Walter Reed Hospital.

The President entered the hospital unannounced. A wedge of Secret Service cleared the path. Aides and staffers followed the President. The entryway went dead quiet. Doctors and nurses still, stone still. A doctor, a lieutenant colonel, ran up to the President and saluted. As a doctor, he rarely had to do that. "Mr. President, are you all right? How can I help."

"You have a US Marshal brought in here, severely wounded. I would like to see him."

"Yes, Sir. He is on the fourth floor. His family and teammates are there."

"Show the way." Said the President.

The group exited the elevator on the fourth floor. Once again, there was stunned silence. The President saw a young woman holding a young boy. They were both crying. As the President approached them, Tower stood and greeted the President.

"Mr. President, you honor us with your presence. "I am Mark Tower; I am the team leader." The President looked at Tower and four other Marshals standing at attention. The Marshal's star, worn around their necks. The President kneeled in front of Mrs. Grace Carpenter. He rubbed the head of the young boy.

"Mrs. Carpenter, I wanted to come here to personally thank you for your husband's courage and offer any help I can for you and your family. If there is anything, anything I can do or anything you might need, please call me. Your husband's extreme courage saved many lives, many innocent families."

Grace Carpenter took the President's hand and continued to cry.

The President looked up, "Who is the chief doctor on this?"

"I am, Mr. President," said a small man in a long white jacket. "Colonel Stephen Hammond."

"Colonel, if there is anything, and I mean anything, you need to save this hero, you will have it. How is he doing?"

"Mr. President, I am surprised he is still alive." The doctor looked at Mrs. Carpenter, making sure she did not hear him. "He has numerous punctures from shrapnel; one lung and his liver were badly damaged, as was a lot of his bowels. He lost a lot of blood, a lot. We are doing all we can; it might not be enough. Time will tell."

"Whatever you need," said the President.

"Tower, walk with me," said the President. They walked to a corner of the room. "What happened?" asked the President.

"Sir?" asked Tower.

"How did you stop the attack? No one knew about it."

"Mr. President, like everyone else, we got the word about the 50 attacks. We were not invited to help." Tower went on to tell how they "guessed" there would be an attack on the US Capitol. How they also guessed what the target might be. "We divided into two groups. My group got lucky or unlucky, looking at Grace Carpenter. We shot two terrorists, but one got the pin out of his grenade. The terrorist was standing in the midst of several families. Carpenter tackled him and fell on the grenade. He saved many people." The President thought for a few moments. "I will make sure his heroism is recognized. When all this insanity is over, I want you to come see me. I have an idea for a special team that you and your men would be ideal for. I'll notify you when I have time. Once again, thank you. The country owes you a great debt."

"Mr. President, there may be a problem." The President stared at Tower in surprise. "During the attack, I saw the Iranian agent, who we believed was the leader of the attack. I confronted him. He reached into his jacket. I thought he might have a grenade or a handgun. As he reached into his jacket, I shot and killed him. He was unarmed; he was reaching for his passport. I shot an unarmed man."

The President smiled. "Don't worry about it, you did well. Your honesty assures me that you are the right man for this special project." The President then went back to quietly talk to Mrs. Carpenter. After half an hour, he left. The Marshals sat with Mrs. Carpenter and her son throughout the night.

Chapter Twenty-Nine

The United States Intelligence Community is made up of 18 agencies under the direction of the Director of National Intelligence. The DNI reports directly to the President. Many of these agencies specialize in a particular form of intelligence collection. The National Reconnaissance Office deals with the collection of intelligence from satellites. The National Security Agency collects SIGINT. Signal Intelligence is collecting from electronic communications. In these agencies, having a top secret clearance is not enough to walk around the office without an escort. All of the military services have intelligence collection capabilities. These range from tactical to strategic. The focal point of military intelligence is the Defense Intelligence Agency. This agency is made up of both military and civilian employees. Despite a misconception, the Central Intelligence Agency is a civilian agency, not a military one.

After the call from the President, the DNI started calling the directors of the 18 agencies. This priority one task would replace the current number one priority. Assets would be tasked. Agents would be told to stop what they were doing and work on this. Satellites would be repositioned to cover Bandar Abbas. Flying a drone or an aircraft over the city would not be allowed or wise. Naval intelligence would analyze the shoreline of the city. If swimmers or landing craft had to go there, they would know the beach gradient and water temperature. The CIA would task assets in the area. Unlike the beloved spy movies, most intelligence personnel can not pass for local citizens. Even those who spoke the language could rarely master the local accents and idioms. Discovery would be disaster. There would be no high-speed chases or fancy tricks to escape. Instead, intelligence agents recruit locals who would have access to the information needed. It was a long process to recruit an asset. Too bad most movies did not show the real procedures. Identifying the motivation of the recruited asset vary. Some help for money, some want asylum. Others do it for revenge, while others do it for ideological reasons. The early identification of the asset's motivation is critical for recruitment.

Each director had their marching orders. They called their deputies, who in turn called their division heads. Within an hour, numerous workers had been called at home and were heading to various offices around the DC area. The lights in numerous buildings came on. The small overnight staff was replaced by the full personnel of the agencies. The President's tasking would be worked on by as many personnel as possible.

It was easy to obtain aerial photography of Mohammed's home and the ports and dock facilities used by his shipping company. The interior of the home was harder to discover. It took checking with local real estate agents on the premise of buying a similar home to get a floor plan. This plan may or may not be the exact dimensions of Mohammed's home. It would be useful for planning purposes. Getting Mohammed's schedule would be harder to obtain. This would require surveillance on his home, his office, and his travel. Again, the movies got it wrong. One person can not do this. No one can follow a person 24 hours a day. Sleep, food, and bathroom breaks would be required. Besides, how do you stay outside someone's home around the clock without alerting them? Once alerted, the schedule might change. Worse, being caught spying in a country such as Iran could result in torture and death. There would be no gentlemanly interrogation. Some of the information could be easily obtained through what is known as open sources. This could be newspapers, magazines, or any information easily obtained from sources open to anyone. One of the first things obtained was a copy of the shipping schedule of the fleet belonging to Mohammad's company.

One of the hardest pieces of information to obtain was Mohammed's mindset. What was he thinking? What would he do next? How far would he go? No satellite could determine this. Unless Mohammed discussed his plans on a cell phone or on the internet, the fanciest signal intelligence equipment could not provide the needed information. This would be the hardest piece of information to obtain and the most critical. This was the area that the CIA excelled in.

There were many people in Iran who did not support the government. They could be easily motivated to provide information that someday might topple the Iranian government. However, the identifying, recruiting, and training of this asset was difficult and complex. You could not just open a school for spies. All this had to be done quietly and away from anyone who might inform on them.

All these efforts, the expensive equipment, the aircraft, the research, could not read Mohammed's mind. Mohammed's mind could not focus. He was angry, angrier than he had ever been. He was frustrated because his plan had failed. True, there were many deaths and injuries, but not nearly enough to cripple the Americans. He needed a new plan. He needed a plan that no one could stop. A plan that he could do on his own. A plan to cripple the Americans beyond their ability to recover from. What could it be? What assets did he have? He was not a soldier. He had no heavy weapons. He was sure he could get some rifles and maybe some small amount of explosives. These would not be even close to what he needed for the massive destruction he wanted. He thought about a major cyber attack on the Americans. However, he did not have the expertise to do this. He did not know anyone who could do this. His frustration grew. He went mad with anger and frustration. He started screaming. He picked up an ashtray and threw it against the wall. He threw the remote for the television against the wall, too. This did not help; he was still mad with rage. He looked around the room. On the mantle and saw a model of one of their cargo ships. He picked it up and was about to smash it against the wall. At the last moment, he stopped. He stared at the model of the ship. He did not move. His mind whirled. The rage disappeared. A smile grew on Mohammed's face. He had the beginning of a plan.

Chapter Thirty

It had been a week since the attacks. The dead, so many of them, were being buried. The wounded were being cared for. Some were in the hospital, while many had gone home. They were scared but happy to be alive and, in many cases, intact. Others were not that lucky. The damage was being repaired and replaced. Shattered windows had been boarded up. Destroyed merchandise had been reordered. The American people had rallied. Their anger demanded that the President not only explain what happened, but what he was going to do about it. The first part was easy. The President addressed the nation. He was on every television network, every radio station, and on numerous streaming networks. The people had the right to know what happened.

He told them. He told them almost everything from the gun smuggling, to the naval gun battle, to a cartel smuggling the terrorist into the United States. He explained the plan and what the goal of the plan was. He showed photos of the attack. He praised the numerous police officers who stopped most of the attacks and the first responders who saved the lives of numerous victims through emergency medical care. He thanked the doctors and nurses who fought to help every victim. He did not tell them two things. The name of the cartel boss who provided the warning about the attack and the price we paid for that information. He also did not tell them the name of the man behind these attacks. He did tell the public that the mastermind was identified and that he could run but not hide from

American vengeance. The President did say vengeance and not justice. This shocked some and pleased others.

The broadcast was also watched in Tehran. The Minister of Intelligence and Security paid attention to every word. He knew of the plot, of course. Arzhang had briefed him on the plan. The Ministry had provided the fifty "freedom fighters" who were willing to sacrifice themselves to destroy America. Everyone knew that since the revolution of 1979, America and Iran would never be friends. Their laws and lifestyles were so far apart that there could not be any meaningful compromise. Once the Shah had been forced out of the country, the strict interpretation of Islamic law controlled the country. The holding of the American Embassy for 444 days showed the world the power of the new government. The failed rescue attempt had both scared and delighted them. Showing parts of American aircraft made them feel more powerful. The Americans killed one of his mid-level managers in Washington, D.C. Arzhang would be branded as a rogue agent. Paperwork was back-dated to show he had been fired weeks before, but he had become mentally unstable. There was no proof to the contrary. Iran had deniability on the world stage. Now, what to do about Mohammad? If he had been successful, he would have been hailed as a hero. The Americans surely knew his identity, even if the American President did not say it during the broadcast. What to do?

Mohammad would be a target for the Americans. Wherever he went, he would be attacked. There was no place safe for him. While the Minister hated America, he knew that they had a long reach. Their spies and other intelligence assets would be looking for Mohammad. They would not stop until he was caught or killed. From the way the American president spoke, capturing him was not high on the list.

The Minister would visit Mohammad. This was not a great idea. It would tie him to Mohammad, but it would give him a face-to-face with the man and maybe figure out how to handle this situation. It would be about a 900-mile trip. His private jet would get him there in two hours. He would land at Bandar Abbas International Airport. From there, it would be a short drive to Mohammad's home. He would have called to make an appointment, but he thought better. He did not want the NSA to listen to the call. He would take his chances.

The flight was uneventful. At the airport, he got a car and drove directly to Mohammad's home. He had been told that Mohammad had been home for several days. He knocked on the door and waited. Mohammad opened the door. He looked terrible. He had not shaved in days; his clothes were dirty and wrinkled. The news of the failure of the operation hit home and hard. "Can I help you?" "The Minister identified himself. "I do not know what happened, I can only guess." "What is your guess?" asked the Minister. "The narcotics criminal in Mexico must have alerted the Americans. They could have easily learned the details of the attack. One of their senior criminals has a son in American custody. Maybe the information was part of the deal?" The Minister thought for a moment. Whatever happened, the events were over and done with. "What are your plans now?" asked the Minister.

Mohammad took a breath. "I will still have my revenge. I will still cripple America. I have worked out a plan. Again, I will fund it and personally lead the attack. My life now only has one purpose."

The Minister thought. This would be a good way to both get rid of Mohammad and make Iran look better in the eyes of the world. While the Minister supported the attacks on America, he had to protect Iran from American and international retaliation. "What is the plan?" asked the Minister.

"With respect, I would rather not say. I am still working out several of the technical details, and I want to be sure no one knows the plan. I will not need help from the government." The Minister would have been offended, but this way, whatever happened, the Iranian government would be in the clear. They honestly had no part in this. "Will the attack be soon?" he asked. "I do not have an exact date, but within a month or six weeks." "Very well," said the Minister. He got up to leave. "I wish you well," He left the home and drove back to the airport for the return flight home. "This should be very interesting, "he thought.

Chapter Thirty-One

The Chairman of the Joints Chiefs had finished reviewing all the plans to take out Mohammad. Based on all the possibilities, he decided to recommend to the President that a special ops team, probably a SEAL team, would go into Bandar Abbas and attempt to capture Mohammad, if possible. If Mohammad resisted, he would be killed and his body removed. The SEALs would probably be inserted by swimming from a submerged submarine. The idea of a HALO jump was considered but rejected. HALO stood for High Altitude Low Opening. This is what civilians call skydiving. Of course, civilians usually do not jump with a hundred pounds of gear, a rifle, night vision goggles, a radio, food, and water. SEALs also usually jump at night. They did not want to be seen on the way down. Mohammad, if captured, would be sedated, fitted with breathing equipment, and either carried or escorted into the water and then guided underwater back to the submarine. There would be a list of agencies that would want to question him.

The Chairman had his staff prepare the usual slide show. All briefings had to have slides. The general and a few aides went out to the parkin got and got onto his assigned vehicle. The drive from the Pentagon to the White House was only a short drive. While en route, he rehearsed his presentation. Then he thought of what possible questions the President could ask and prepared an answer for each. All good briefers did this. Figure out what could be asked and then prepare an answer. Saying, "I'll check and get back to you," was not the way to be known as a good briefer. Careers could be made or broken by the briefer's ability.

The car drove up to the White House checkpoint. All the people in the car were on the security access roster. They still had to show their identification card. The photo on the identification card was carefully compared to the person presenting it. The Secret Service took its job very seriously.

The car was parked, and the Chairman and his group exited the vehicle and entered the White House. They walked past the Marine guard. General Harper, an Army officer, always admired the Marine's uniform. A perfect fit, not a wrinkle or blemish. The Marine saluted the general. A perfect salute as usual. Once inside, the general and his aides were escorted into the Oval Office. People don't just wander around the White House, not even four-star generals.

General Harper exchanged pleasantries with the President. Then the briefing started. The President listened closely. The reason for a ground mission as opposed to a strike by either aircraft or ships. The reason for selecting SEALs by sea rather than HALO was discussed. The other options were also discussed. It was better to tell why those options were discarded than wait to be asked. When the briefing was over, the President thought for a few moments. "Tell the CENTCOM Commander to get a team ready to go. When the DNI has a concrete time when Mohammad would be home, you can give them the go signal." Harper and his party stood; the meeting was over. The aides carried the briefing material. The general came to attention and saluted his Commander-in-Chief. He then turned and headed for the door.

"Harper," said the President.

The general stopped and turned to face the President. "Get the bastard."

"Yes, sir, Mr. President," the general answered back.

Harper exited the White House and walked to his vehicle. He opened the front passenger door and sat down. Long ago, Harper had told his folks not to open the door for him. "I am fully capable of opening my own door." Harper did not need to have a soldier act as a doorman. Back at the Pentagon, Harper called the CENTCOM commander on a secure phone.

"Sean, this is Bill Harper. How are you?" Admiral Sean Harris, the four-star commander of CENTCOM, replied that he was fine. He knew this was not a social call. "I need you and your folks to plan a hostile extraction from Bandar Abbas. The President has authorized the op. Capture if you can, kill if you cannot." "Is this the guy who masterminded the terrorist attack?" asked the Admiral. "Sure is." "The DNI will provide you with the intel you need." "We will be ready," said Harris. Harper thanks the Admiral. He knew Harris would make sure every possible option would be prepared for. If the op could be done, Harris would get it done.

Harper put in a call to the DNI top to let him know that the President approved the op and that Admiral Harris was waiting on the intelligence package. The DNI told Harper he already knew about the approval. "We are working around the clock to get his schedule and the layout of his house. We are also pinpointing any defenses in the area." Harper thanked the DNI and hung up.

Now, everyone would wait for the intelligence that would trigger this operation in a hostile country for the most wanted man in America. Not everyone waited. Mohammad did not have to wait. He did not need approval. He did not need funding or Congressional Oversight. He had the will and the funds. He sat at his work desk and made a list of equipment he would need. Almost all of it he already had. He just needed some electronic equipment. He knew where to get these devices. When you are rich, you can buy almost anything. He could not bring his father back. Now thousands of Americans would pay. He would kill many and disrupt their economy for years. He would light up the sky. All would know the price of losing his father. He was grateful to the man who killed his father's so-called friend. The one who really started all this. That was not enough. His hatred knew no limits. He would do whatever it took to complete this plan. He went back to making his list of needed equipment.

Chapter Thirty-Two

While the Intelligence Community was busy trying to develop enough intelligence to target Mohammad, he was developing his plan of attack. Satellites flew over his home several times a day. They looked for any changes, any activity. A ship stationary outside the territorial waters of Iran listened in to his telephone and his Wi fi. That was not enough. CIA had several resources in the area. They could not get into his home or his place of work. The office was large and near the piers. One did get to see him leaving in the evenings. He could not sit outside the office for long. Suspicious activity in Iran was met with a strong police presence. This could not happen.

Mohammad, in his office, called in his chief engineer. The man had worked on ships since he was 14 years old. He had learned about every section and aspect of the ships. He could go from wiring the communications to changing parts on the engine. "I need you to modify three of our ships," said Mohammad. He showed the modifications he wanted to his engineer.

The man looked at the diagrams. He studied them carefully. "Why would you want this? It would be a lot of work, and it really doesn't serve any purpose," said the engineer.

Mohammad smiled and nodded. "I know, but trust me, I will need these changes. How long do you think it will take?"

The engineer thought for several moments. "If I can get the equipment and the men to do the work, maybe a week or two." "I will get you the electronic equipment. I think you can get the rest of the materials on the pier. As far as the men are concerned, I will offer a bonus for those who will work on it. An extra bonus if the work is completed within a week." The engineer picked up the diagrams and left the office. He would start getting the material today. Mohammad knew this would be his last chance for revenge. And what revenge it would be.

The DNI reviewed all the incoming intelligence reports on Mohammad. He was getting daily calls from the President and the Chairman of the Joint Chiefs. The intelligence was needed. The Chairman actually needed the information more. The Chairman would pass the intelligence to CENTCOM. CENTCOM would pass it to the Special Operations Command Central. SOCCENT would pass the information to the team tasked with the mission. Once the team got the information, they would start the detailed planning needed for the mission into a hostile country. Equipment was needed tailored to the mission. They needed to get a submarine to transport them to the waters near the Iranian beach. Some submarines were better suited for underwater delivery of special operations personnel. The President did not need the detailed information. However, he was the President. There was still not enough intelligence for detailed planning. He would have to press harder for the intelligence. He could not press too hard.

Intelligence comes at its own time or with a stroke of luck. This mission was too important to be done incorrectly.

Mohammad's engineer had gotten all the required equipment within 48 hours. He had to pay top dollar for the equipment, but Mohammad didn't mind. It took Mohammad 3 days to get the required electronic equipment. He got strange looks for the special order. Once again, money greased the wheels for the sale. The engineer would install the equipment and the electronics. He and his workers worked 12-hour days. The items had to be installed correctly. They were not designed to be used this way. He could not understand why Mohammad wanted this. It made no sense. He was the boss, however. The engineer had worked for Mohammad's father and now for Mohammad. His loyalty was beyond question.

The DNI called the Director of the CIA on a secure phone. "What's the holdup? The military really needs that information for proper planning. "I have every Iranian asset working on it. Mohammad's home is like a walled fortress. The 10-foot solid wall around the house blocks any view. Mohammad's phone calls were all very unremarkable. His office was not secured, but any person entering the grounds had to go through a checkpoint. Our assets cannot get in there. The asset has parked outside on a public street to see what time Mohammad came and went. He comes and goes at different times each day. No pattern could be detected." The DNI ran his hand through his short hair. The CIA was doing the best they could. It just was not enough. "The lack of intelligence will delay the operation. I would hate to send a team in blind. That could be disaster." The CIA Director said he would push for more data. He hoped this would not compromise his assets. Sometimes fate has good timing. Within an hour, the DNI got a phone call. Satellite imagery had shown unusual work going on at the docks. The work went on until late at night and once until early in the morning. The details of the activity would be analyzed, and a report would be ready shortly.

The engineer told Mohammad that the electronics had been installed. He needed one more day to make sure it worked properly. A test run in open water would be needed. The other equipment had been installed. It worked fine. It was a simple installation, even though the equipment was not normally installed this way. Another day or so, everything would be ready. He started the final planning and scheduling. This is going to work. Every detailed had been worked out. Every loose end had been considered and planned for. Vengeance was at hand. After this was over, he did not know what he would do. It didn't matter to him if he lived or died. This thought actually empowered him. He could not be stopped. He could not be hurt. His life only had one purpose now.

Chapter Thirty-Three

U.S. Navy Senior Chief Robert Evans was in the exercise room lifting weights. Each lift generated a grunt. He strained, and the veins in his arms bulged. Sweat dripped from his face and chest. Other members of his SEAL team were also working out. They had come to the weight room after their morning run. They ran early in the morning to beat the desert heat. Bahrain had a great beach. Their morning five-mile run took them past numerous high-rise buildings. Staying in peak shape was a requirement. No one knew when they might be called or where they had to go. There was no time to get in shape.

Commander Morgan entered the room and approached Evans.

"Senior Chief, looks like you are going to have a mission. I don't have all the details yet, but it will be a kill/capture mission in Iran. We are waiting for more intelligence before the order is given."

"Iran? They are not very friendly to us," he joked.

"Who is the target?"

"The guy who planned the terror attack on the 4th. He is back in Iran. He is in his hometown of Bandar Abbas. He runs a huge shipping company from there. His father was killed several months ago when one of their ships was running guns and tried to take on a destroyer."

Evans nodded. "I'll get the team on it this morning. Any idea of when we are going?

"No," answered Morgan. We are waiting for an intelligence update. I'll make sure you have all we have on him up to now," Evans knew it was going to be a long day.

Later that morning, Evans had assembled his team in their secure area, safe from prying eyes and ears. He told them about the mission.

"Do we have to capture him? It would be a lot safer and easier just to kill him. He is responsible for hundreds of dead Americans and a lot more wounded," asked Petty Officer Washington. "Why risk our lives so he can have a trial on the taxpayer's dime?"

"Good question," replied Evans. "One, he may have a lot of intel about Iranian operations in the US. Two, because we were told to do it that way."

There was a slow nodding of heads. It was obvious that Washington's idea was shared by the others. "Of course, if there is resistance, we must protective ourselves." A smile appeared on the faces of several of the team members.

"I have maps of the area, photos of the target's home and office, and of course, the target himself. We are waiting for an update on his schedule. No sense going in if he is not home. You know what needs to be done, so get on in. I have to see a man about a submarine." They all laughed, and Evans left the room.

Evans went to Commander Morgan's office. He knocked and entered. SEALs are less formal about rank than the surface Navy.

"Boss, I've got the guys working on a plan. I guess we will swim to the beach from an underwater sub. Do we have a sub available?"

Morgan shook his head, "I can't ask for one until the ops is approved. Just keep planning as best you can."

At the same time this was happening, Mohammad was inspecting several modified ships at his dock. He made sure all the electronic equipment was properly installed and fully functional. The installation of the metal cranes and the other items was complete. Their functions were tested and retested. He may or may not survive this. If he didn't, it would not be because he didn't check on everything. Loading the small, but powerful boats on the decks of several tanker ships took an effort. Huge cranes were used. The tanker ships were not designed to carry these boats. Mounting the large crane on either side of the boat took work. While these cranes would lower the smaller boats into the water. It would, of course, reduce the capacity of the ship noticeably.

Mohammad went to his office and got out a large number of navigational maps. He carefully planned the routes for his ships. He calculated the distance and time required to get from his dock to his targets. He wanted the ships to arrive at the different locations at the same time. Or at least as close as possible. He had to consider the sea conditions. The small boats would not fare well in heavy seas. This took a lot of planning. Mohammad was more than capable of doing the calculations. Just took some time.

It took him all night. He reviewed the course, the weather, and the predicted sea conditions. He left nothing to chance. He selected men whom he trusted totally and who were more than capable of performing the mission. They had worked for his father and now for him. Their loyalty was beyond question. He calculated what time they would leave and in what order. All that was left to do was to load the ships with their cargo. Once that was done, he would allow his men to go home and be with their families. The mission should go smoothly, but one never knows. He owed his men that much.

The satellite that flew across the dark sky saw the activity on the dock. It took a series of high-resolution photos. These pictures were digitized and sent back to Earth. Once downloaded, they were printed out. They would be immediately reviewed and interpreted. The analyst on duty that night knew these photos had the highest priority. All other photos from all over the world would wait. He examined the photos with different magnifying equipment. The photos were of very high quality. He could zoom in and see if he was on the roof of the office on the peer. At first, he was confused. The configuration of the ships was quite different from what he was used to. There was nothing way out of the ordinary, but still. To equip the ships in this manner, well, he had never seen that before. Why were some of the ships being loaded in the middle of the night? Closer examination showed more workers on the dock than was normal in the daytime, let alone in the middle of the night. He called for the duty officer. He knew these photos had meaning; he just did not know what it was.

Chapter Thirty-Four

Paul Hernandez had been an image interpretation specialist for the U.S. Air Force. He had graduated from a highly specialized course and had served on active duty in both Europe and Hawaii. He got tired of travelling and left the Air Force. He was offered a job with the National Geospatial-Intelligence Agency in Virginia. He liked Virginia. Four seasons, rolling hills, rivers, and an ocean. There was something for everyone there. Washington, D.C. was very close, with all its museums, monuments, and National Zoo. In a very expensive area to live, these tourist areas were all free.

Hernandez waited for the duty officer. Sarah Jones approached him. She had worked there for over ten years. She worked her way up by talent, not by favoritism. She knew her stuff.

"OK, Paul, what do you have?" Hernandez showed her the new photos.

"They usually closed at dark. Sometimes a few men worked on a ship due to leave in the morning. These photos show more folks working at night than in the daytime. There were several ships, two or three, hard to tell, showing the kind of cranes used to lower boats, being installed. These types of cranes were never installed on cargo ships. They take up too much room, cutting profits."

Jones placed the pictures on the large screen at Hernandez's station. She zoned in and then zoned in further. She stared at the ships. Hernandez had a good eye; something was going on.

Jones passed the information up the chain of command. Normally, this might have taken days, but due to the DNI's priority message, it got to the Chairman of the Joint Chiefs within two hours. The Chairman got the pictures. It was good to have a secure computer on his desk. He looked at the pictures and then called Jones directly. He did not have the time to go through the chain of command. Jones picked up her phone when it rang. She was not expecting what she heard. "Ms. Jones, this is General Harper. I got the photos you sent. I am not an expert. What is going on?" Jones was not used to talking to such senior people. She usually went to her boss, who went to his boss, until the information finally got to where it was supposed to be.

"Sir, General, the photos show several ships being modified with various."

"Jones," the general interrupted, "Give me the short down and dirty, no bullshit answer. This is not a briefing. What the hell is going on in these photos?" She took a breath; there goes her career. "General, there are four large tankers being readied to sail. They are being prepared at an unusually fast pace. All four ships are being fitted with the kind of crane used to pull boats out of the water and put them on the deck of the ship. The boats could hold several people, probably no more than ten each. These boats could operate in the ocean as well as in a large body of water, such as a sea. The four main ships should be ready to sail in about 24 hours or so. These ships are also being loaded with what looks like fuel. Not fuel for the ship, but fuel as if it were going to supply a major refinery." She waited. She hoped she had not struck her foot in it.

"Jones, I want you and your team, if you have a team, to come to my office right now. Tell your boss to provide you with transportation. I do not want any of your higher folks to come with you. This is going to be a down-and-dirty meeting. There are some folks I want you to tell this to."

"Yes, sir." Said Jones.

"Jones, said Harper, "Great job."

Jones ran to her boss and told him about the phone call. She needed a car to go to the Pentagon. Hernandez was gathering up all their data to bring with them. Jones had to tell her boss twice that the Chairman only wanted to see her and Hernandez, not the hierarchy of the agency. Feeling his missed his chance to meet the Chairman, he ordered a car and driver to take her to the Pentagon. They went outside to the vehicle. The driver, who was probably armed, opened the door for them. His job was to get them through traffic and safeguard the Top Secret information during the trip. Jones and Hernandez reviewed their findings while the car raced into D.C.

At the Pentagon, the driver stayed with the vehicle. Armed security from outside agencies was usually not received well. Jones and Hernandez entered the Pentagon. Guards made sure there was nothing unauthorized in their briefcases. As a member of the Intelligence Community, their ID badges would get them into the building. They were escorted to the Chairman's office. The Pentagon had its own way of labeling offices. There were five sides, obviously. Each side had several corridors, and each one of these had levels both above and below the ground. It was easy to get lost.

Once at the Chairman's outer office, they were immediately let into his private office. They expected to see the Chairman. They were surprised to see an admiral and an Air Force general. "Have a seat," said the Chairman. They both sat very nervously. When they were in the service, even a one-star general was a big deal. Here were three four-star officers and someone in civilian clothes. They did not recognize the CIA representative. "I want you to tell us what you told me before. I also want your honest, unedited opinion about what is going on."

Hernandez and Jones looked at each other. This would make or break their careers. Worse, it could lead to some kind of military action. Hopefully, the right kind. Jones took a breath and looked at the Chairman.

"The Abu al-Fadi shipyards have been in operation for several decades. They are considered a legitimate shipping line. They serve mostly the Middle East but do have activities in the United States, Europe, and Asia. The long-running owner, Bijan Abu al-Fadi, was killed recently in a sea battle with a Navy destroyer."

"Yes, we know that. What do you have to add? What is going on in the shipyards? asked the Chairman in a slightly frustrated voice.

Jones composed herself. "The yard normally has 1 or 2 ships being serviced and loaded at any one time. For the last few days, satellites have picked up four ships being readied for departure. All four ships have been modified to have a side hoist installed. This hoist could lower a boat into the sea or bring it back on board. The side of the crane indicates that the boat could be big enough to hold almost a dozen people, counting the crew. The boats would be capable of being seaworthy in an ocean. The other activity, which we noticed," she said, looking at Hernandez, "was that all four ships are being loaded with fuel on their decks and cargo areas. This could mean an expensive delivery somewhere, or just trying to extend the range of the ships. It is hard to know the exact amount of fuel on each ship, but it could be as much as one and a half times their normal load. What made this unusual was that while the fuel was being loaded on board, crews were welding the hoists onto the deck of the ship. This is not normal and extremely dangerous. Crews are also working 18-hour days instead of the normal 10 to 12-hour workday."

"Okay," said the Chairman, "what is your best guess as to what is going on?"

Hernandez jumped in; Jones was obviously getting stressed. "Sir, we believe that all four ships will sail in the next 2 or 3 days. That they can reach anywhere in the world without stopping to refuel. That the amount of fuel has no normal function. It is excessive. This operation, whatever it is, cost the company a huge amount of money, which would not be compensated by the delivery of the fuel. There is no normal reason for the four ships to be equipped with these hoists. I expect the small boats to be secured on the tankers within the next 24 hours."

The Chairman looked at the other people in the room. "Thank you for your candid evaluation. Please wait outside for a few minutes." Jones and Hernandez nodded and exited the room. They sat in some chairs and tried to slow their breathing. What is going on?

The Chairman looked at the others in the room. The CIA representative started. "The killing of his father has driven the son, Mohammad, out of his mind. Reports say he is driving his workers at an insane pace. This is not like him. I do not believe those ships are being set up for a standard fuel delivery. I think we must expect some kind of terror attack with them. I have no idea where or how, but we must watch those ships 24/7, lest they head somewhere without our knowing about it."

The Air Force Chief of Staff agreed. "We need satellite coverage around the clock. We have a few AWAC aircraft that can watch them for a while, but it is a big ocean. Our aircraft should not enter Iranian airspace. The politicians would have a fit. We can have some in the air within an hour or so and do in-flight refueling to keep them up. If the ships travel together, that would make it easier for all of us. We must assume they will split up once they leave the port."

The Chief of Naval Operations, the senior uniformed officer in the Navy, smiled. "We can use submarines to shadow them once they are at sea. While the E-2C Hawkeye can see about half the range of the Air Force AWACS, we can rotate them off a carrier in the region. We have fleets in the Atlantic and Mediterranean which can monitor these ships. If we have to, we can stop them." "They would have to violate some international law first?" asked the Chairman. "Well, yes, but we can safely monitor them until that time."

The Chairman called Jones and Hernandez back into the room. "Until you hear otherwise from me, your sole duty is to monitor those 4 ships. I expect around-the-clock coverage. Reallocate satellites if you have to. I will clear it with your agency head. You may be stopping a terrorist attack on the US. I am not sure, but you will help us find out. You will report anything, and I mean anything that happens at that boat yard. If the ships move, I expect a call at any time, day or night, without hesitation. You will call me directly. Tell me what is happening, while it is happening. Do you both understand?"

"Yes, sir," they answered at the same time.

"Go back to your desks and get to work. This should only be a few days. Here is my direct phone number, use it! "Harper handed them both a business card with his direct phone number on it. They exited the room. They were escorted back to their waiting car. Their hearts were still racing when they got back to their desks.

The Air Force general sent an alert to CENTCOM, as did the admiral, notifying key units to be on alert. That reconnaissance aircraft was to be ready to fly a mission. What the mission was, was not explained at that time. Those warships not actively engaged were to reposition themselves to be able to monitor the Gulf of Oman and the Persian Gulf. The target or targets would be identified as soon as possible.

Chapter Thirty-Five

Mohammad checked his math once again. There would be no room for error. Everything was being taken into account. At first, he thought the ships should sail together, like a small fleet. This would be impressive. It would also provide security from pirates. Yes, sad to say, there were still pirates operating in international waters. Almost all ship captains were ordered not to fight back, just surrender the ship in hopes of the crew getting home safely. Mohammad thought this was stupid. Why just hand over a billion-dollar ship and its cargo in the hopes that some criminal would be kind? Nonsense. Mohammad made sure there were enough weapons on board each of these ships to repel any pirate attack. Now, a military ship was another matter. His father had learned that the hard way. He selected different routes for the ships. Two ships would go through the Suez Canal, through the Mediterranean, and into the Atlantic through the Straits of Gibraltar. From there, they would separate and go to their targets. The other two ships would go the long way around. From Iran, southwest to take the old route, around Africa. After passing Cape Town, they would turn northwest and head to their targets. This would be a long trip. These ships would leave first. He wanted all the ships to be on target at the same time. While probably not at the same minute, at least on the same day. This would enhance the effect of the attack and force the Americans to spread their forces out in any attempt to stop him. American would burn, and he would see it happen.

He had to pick a good day for the attack. His original idea of the 4th of July would have been a great day for an attack. The attack had gone off on time, but with limited results. Worse, the American news media did not play up the attacks by showing the death and destruction. They were more interested in music and fireworks. He would give them fireworks. The ships were ready. All that was needed was for the crews to board the ships and get underway. They had already been stocked with food and water. Of course, they would have weapons to defend themselves from pirates. Nothing must stop the mission. Mohammad looked out of his window at the water. All he ever wanted was to run the business with his father. They had worked so hard; now their labors were for death and not building. Then it struck him, Labor Day. Another American holiday. A time when everyone was not working and having a good time. He would make sure it was not a good day for the Americans. His target date was now set.

Even as the finally preparations were being made by Mohammed, the American Intelligence Community focused on Bandar Abbas. Jones and Hernandez, with their new authority, had "repurposed" several extra satellites to watch the dock area and to be ready, as best as possible, to follow the ships when they sailed. One of them called the Chairman every eight hours with an update. Once something started to happen, these calls would be much more frequent. The SEAL team under Senior Chief Evans was ready to go, but their limited intelligence made this trip into a very hostile country seem very dangerous and, worse than that, likely to fail. Like a coiled spring, they waited for the word. The Chairman had worked around the clock. He had coordinated with the Intelligence Community, the Department of Homeland Security, the FBI, and the President. The President, at first, wanted hourly updates. When the response was, "Nothing new," the updates became every two hours, and then every four. Neither official liked having their work interpreted by calls that accomplished nothing. The calls were now, "As soon as anything happens." The American military was ready. Military bases were not put on full alert, as their readiness posture could alert a foreign intelligence service. The Air Force had repositioned their aerial refueling tankers to help reconnaissance aircraft extend their range. Naval ships and submarines spread out. The better to cover more area, and if necessary, take action. The stage was set.

Mohammad walked each ship. He checked and double-checked the equipment and the readiness of each ship. The electronic equipment was working perfectly. He had personally checked the equipment. He also checked the status of each of the smaller boats, which were mounted in the middle of each of the three ships. He checked the crane, which would lower the boats into the water. He went to the fourth ship and checked the crane, which would hoist up the smaller boats. He made sure there was enough room to recover the boats onto the fourth ship. On a worst-case basis, he could easily recover the three crews and boats. He really didn't care about the boats, but it made the crew happy to know there was a plan for their survival. This was not a suicide mission. Only the Americans needed to die. Not his people. Tomorrow, the first two ships would sail. Several days later, the other two ships would sail. He would be part of that group. He had full trust in his crews and their leaders. This mission must not, could not fail. Tonight would be a night of prayer and feasting.

Chapter Thirty-Six

The next morning, the crews of the two ships went on board. They took their duty position and waited for the order to go. They did not have to wait long. Mohammad walked out on to the pier. He looked up and saw the captain of the first ship, the Prophet. They made eye contact and waved at him. That was the signal to proceed. The captain started barking orders. The engines came alive and the mooring lines were untied and retracted. After several minutes, the huge ship started to move away from the pier. Slowly at first, and then moving noticeably into the open water. Mohammad walked down the pier to the second ship, the Lion. Once again, he made eye contact with the ship's captain, who was standing on the bridge. The same hand wave was given and the procedure started again on this ship. Mohammad looked at both ships with pride. His father would be avenged by the ships that his father had purchased and by the crews that he had trained. The ships started to pick

up speed. They were now obviously moving away from the pier and the port. No one gave them a second look. While it was unusual for two ships to leave at the same time, it did happen. There were several other companies which used the dock area. They would also have ships coming and going. Afterall, Bandar Abbas was a port city and no one would pay any attention.

No one except Jones and Hernandez. Satellites saw the ships leave the dock. The images show the ships picking up speed and traveling south. The images allowed Jones and Hernandez to calculate the speed of the ships. As the ships moved out, Hernandez started to reposition satellites to be able to follow the ships. This would take time. Hopefully the ships would not change course too quickly. There were only so many satellites that could cover the area. Jones was on the phone. She called the Chairman's office. After a moment, she was transferred directly to the Chairman.

"Sir, two ships are moving. They have just left the dock. The other two ships have not moved."

"Thank you," said the Chairman. "Any idea where they are going?"

"No, sir, they just pulled away from the dock, within the last 10 minutes."

"Great work, keep me advised." The Chairman hung up and called three other four star officers. The Chief of Staff of the Air Force, the Chief of Naval Operations and the CENTCOM Commander were briefed on the ship's movement. "We need to follow those ships and be ready to follow the other two ships, if and when the sail," said the Chairman. The Chief of Naval Operations asked, "We have a problem with attacking these ships in international waters. We do not know their real intent. Remember the uproar made for sinking a small drug boat? "These things are a city block long and carry enough fuel to cause a major environmental crisis. What are the rules of engagement?"

"Good question," said the Chairman. "I have legal looking into it right now. We are also trying to get an off the record opinion from a Supreme Court Judge. I doubt we will get it, but it is worth a try. We hope the CIA will let us know their intent and how they are armed. We need to know and not guess before we pull the trigger." The uncertainty of the situation bothered everyone. How do you give orders when you are not sure yourself? "Let's hope the intel folks come up with something. We do not know if they are headed here or some other country. We need more information. Until then monitor them as best you can." After some head shaking, the conference call ended. The Chairman could feel a headache coming on.

The two ships sailed at a normal speed. The ship would travel at about 18 knots, about 20 mph. 24 hours a day. It would take them weeks to get to their targets. About an hour after they left the port, the two ships started to separate. They would sail about fifty miles apart. This would make them look like every other cargo tanker. It would also make it much more difficult for intelligence or military assets to follow them. They would sail on the course that Mohammad had planned for them. They were excited that they would be part of a major attack on America. They were also happy that this was not a suicide mission. At least it was not supposed to be. The brilliance of Mohammad in planning the attack and their escape was truly remarkable. No one would be able to guess their plan.

CENTCOM assets would look for the ships. An AWACS picked them up sailing past the coast of Oman. A Navy ship picked them up approaching the Somali coast. Their course and speed were totally normal. There was nothing to alert them about anything out of the ordinary. Satellites were repositioned to follow them. There was nothing to give them any idea of the destination of the ships. There were many questions, but few answers. The ships continued on. While 50 miles apart, the ships were between Kenya and the Seychelles. The weather was good. The ship's captains were hoping for at least clouds or fog to help hide them. They were told that there was a good chance that the American would be looking for them. They had done nothing wrong and should be left alone.

Jones and Hernandez were working around the clock to task satellites to follow the ships. They were not as easy to move around as they were on television. Jones wished that the Air Force had kept the SR-71 aircraft. While they were expensive to maintain, they could move at speeds no other aircraft could match. They could be refueled in midair to extend their range. It had been flown from New York to London in under two hours. Commercial airliners take almost 7 hours. They could exceed 2,000 miles per hour. If she only had one. There was a lot of ocean out there. Jones had coordinated with other intelligence agencies. The largest American intelligence agency, the National Security Agency wasn't much help. The ships at sea did not use their radios or even their satellite phones. There was nothing to listen to. Numerous assets were directed at the dock area and Mohammad's home. They heard nothing but normal conversations. Either there was nothing going on, or Mohammad was a very careful man. The CIA did everything they could to recruit a local man in Bandar Abbas. Unlike movies, spies do not wear fancy suits and sneak into denied areas. People who normally have access to the information needed are recruited to obtain the needed information. The agent doing the recruiting look for weaknesses in the subject. Money, blackmail, asylum and ideology were some of the motivations used. The recruitment is not overnight. Information was needed now.

Colonel Hugh Laskin had been a lawyer for twenty-five years and had served in the Army for over twenty years. He had served in a variety of assignments in numerous countries around the world. During the fighting in Iraq, he had been in a remote village investigating a possible criminal offense by a solider. While there, the village was attacked by a large enemy force. Several Army soldiers had been killed and several more wounded. Laskin had left the relative safety of the command post. He ran to a wounded soldier, picked him up and ran with him back to the command post, where there were medics. He then ran out again, and carried back another wounded soldier. At this point, reinforcements arrived and pushed the enemy back. After several months, the CENTCOM Commander decorated Laskin with the Silver Star for heroism.

Today, Laskin was waiting outside the office of the Chairman of the Joint Chiefs. He was prepared to brief the Chairman on the legal aspects of the situation. After several minutes, the general's aide showed the colonel in to the Chairman's office.

"Okay, Hugh, where do we stand?"

"Sir, we have a problem. We know this guy orchestrated the 4th of July attacks. We cannot prove it. The only witness to the Mexican deployment was dead. Even if he was alive, the testimony of a drug lord doesn't carry much weight. He would come across in any court as an injured person. His father killed by the Navy. Dad had no record of any anti-US activities. Mohammad was not even in the US when the attacks occurred. No proof at all. Now we have at least two ships sailing. The company regularly sails ships to various countries around the world. Again, no proof. We have no proof that anything illegal about these ships. We have suspicion, but no proof. The two ships, as best I can find out, are traveling through international waters. They are not breaking any laws. We have no concrete information that the ships are doing anything wrong. We have no right to stop, let alone attack these ships."

The Chairman thought for a moment. "Is there anything we can do?"

"For right now, all we can do is follow, monitor the ships, and hope we can find some evidence of terrorism. Until then, legally we cannot do anything else. "Laskin saluted, picked up his papers and left the office. Nothing like telling the top general that he was powerless to protect the country from a possible terrorist attack. He told the truth. That was all he could do.

The two ships continued sailing. They were now between Mozambique and Madagascar. The crew had more than enough food and water. There was not much in the way of entertainment. The use of a cell phone, tablet or computer was not allowed. No electronic signature for the Americans to follow.

Chapter Thirty-Seven

It had been a week since the first two ships left the dock. Mohammad knew it was time for the second phase of the operation to start. He gave the order and the two crews got on their ships. The ships were called the Wind and the Light. These two ships were almost identical to the first two ships which left a week ago. The only difference was that the Light did not have the small boat on it that the other ships had. This is the ship which Mohammad would sail on. He would control the attack and hopefully the recovery of his men after the attack. These ships also were stocked with drinking water and food for the trip. The Light had extra food and water on her, more so than the other three ships. When the captains signaled that they were ready to sail, Mohammad waved at the captain of the Wind. The captain returned the wave. The lines securing the ship to the dock were released. The ship's engines started up. The ship slowly moved away from the dock.

Mohammad watched the ship move away from the dock. He then walked to the Light and walked up the ramp. The captain saluted him. "Captain, set sail." He used an old sailing term, even those there was not a sail on the ship. The lines were released. The engine came to life. Slowly the ship moved away from the dock. Mohammad stood on the bow of the ship. He watched the Wind sail directly in front of them. They would travel together until they entered the Mediterranean. This was perfectly normal. They would sail past Oman and Yemen before they would turn north into the Red Sea and then on to the Suez Canal. This was an everyday route used by dozens of ships. They could not hide, but they would not raise any suspicion.

The telephone rang. It was 2:30 AM. General Harper rolled over and cursed. He had been sound asleep. He was standing in a beautiful Alaskan stream. The weather was wonderful. He had just hooked a huge salmon. Life was good. Then the telephone brought him back to reality.

"Harper," he said.

"Sir, it's Jones. I wanted to let you know that the other two ships have just sailed. Within the last 30 minutes. They are sailing together but that is normal when leaving the port." She hated to wake him at this time, but he did say anytime 24/7.

"Anything unusual seen?" asked Harper.

"No, sir," said Jones. "Well sir, the number of crew members does seem a little short. There are enough of the crew to properly sail the ship, but not enough to efficiently unload their cargo, whatever it might be."

"Any idea why?" asked Harper.

"No, sir," answered Jones.

"Okay, keep me updated and let me know when you figure out where they are going."

"Yes, sir," said Jones.

"And Jones," said Harper, "good job." "Thank you, sir." He hung up the phone and wondered that the hell this Mohammad had in mind.

An Air Force AWACS aircraft picked up the two ships. They were making 20 knots and passing Muscat. Nothing unusual here, but the position, course and speed were reported. CENTCOM did it's best to monitor the course of the four ships. There were breaks in the coverage. The ocean is vast. However, between planes, ships and satellites, the general course could be plotted. There was no idea of where the ships were headed or what they would do when they got there. There are a lot of frustrated people trying to solve this puzzle.

Mohammad looked to his right and saw the coast of Yemen. Once they got past Yemen, they would turn north from the Gulf of Aden and travel through the Red Sea. These were calm waters and the weather was beautiful. Maybe this was a sign? He was not sure he believed in this type of thing, but he would gladly accept it.

They sailed on, day after day. They had just passed Djibouti on their port side and were approaching Assab in Eritrea when it happened. Mohammad saw the two small boats approaching they at high speed. These were not US Navy boats. He got a pair of binoculars and studied them. Pirates, he thought. May they be cursed. His ships would not be scared or intimidated. He would not allow his ships to be boarded. Not only was this insulting, but it also would slow down their progress. "Captain," he yelled, all ahead full, signal the Wind to do the same. We will not be boarded." As the two high speed boats approached them, he could see they had some sort of assault rifles and rocket propelled grenades. His ships and crew would not bow down to these thugs.

"Everyone, get a weapon. Prepare to repel boarders," Mohammed yelled. The crew ran to a locker inside the ship's bridge. The captain had unlocked it. Each man grabbed an assault rifle except for two men who grabbed RPGs. "Captain, signal the Wind to defend themselves," said Mohammad. As the fast boats closed on the tanker ships, each captain increased the speed of the ship to its maximum safe speed. The two fast boats closed on the ships from the rear. A man, standing on the lead boat, waved at them and yelled something. Mohammad ignored him. The man pointed an assault rifle at Mohammad. Mohammad ignored him. The man fired a burst at the ship. The bullets struck the Light, causing no damage. Mohammad would not allow this stupidity to interfere with his plan. He gave the order and a dozen men on the Light opened fire on the lead boat. One of the men fired an RPG at the boat. Between the gunfire and the RPG, the boat exploded. Bodies were tossed into the sea. Mohammad doubted there were any survivors and he di not care. Let their friends pick them up, if they wanted to.

The second boat accelerated past the Light and pulled alongside the Wind. The captain of the Wind ignored the boat. Nine men on the deck of the Wind stood and pointed their weapons at the small boat. The pirate made a wise decision and moved away from the huge ship. The pirates headed for land. The attack was over. There had been no damage to the ships and none of Mohammad's men were hurt. They would continue on the mission.

The encounter did not go unnoticed. Both aerial and shipboard radar picked up some kind of disturbance in the area. This would have gone unnoticed, except for the CENTCOM wide alert. A US Navy Oliver Hazzard Perry class frigate was directed to the area. They found the wreckage of the small boat and the remains of the crew. They were all dead, floating in the water. This too was sent immediately to CENTCOM. CENTCOM forward the information to the Joint Chiefs.

The Chief of Naval Operations and his chief intelligence officer, Vice Admiral Morton, walked over to the Chairman's office. It was a short walk inside the Pentagon. They presented Harper with the latest information. "It appears that the two ships in question were attacked by pirates. This is not uncommon in this area. What is uncommon is that the two ships fought back and fought back hard. The small boat was blown to bits. This was not from just rifle fire." Harper asked, "Does this give us a legal reason to stop these ships?" "No, sir," said Morton. "They were defending themselves while under armed attack. International law allows for this. What is unusual is that most ships just stop, give them some kind of payment or tribute and sail on. The tanker ship crew were heavily armed and engaged the pirates. This also is legal. They have not reported the incident as of yet, but this is also not illegal." "So, we know where they are, what direction the are going and little else?" asked Harper. The admirals just nodded.

The next week or so passed without incident. The first two ships had sailed past Cape Town and were heading into the South Atlantic. They were now over one hundred miles apart and heading for their targets. The Wind and the Light were approaching Gibraltar. It was common knowledge that several countries had intelligence assets on Gibraltar. It took little effort to see any surface ship passing between the Atlantic Ocean and the Mediterranean Sea. As the passage way was only about 8 miles wide, one did not need fancy spy equipment to monitor the passage. A pair of binoculars or a camera with a decent lens could identify any surface ship passing through. The Strait was deep, ranging from about 1,000 feet to almost 3,000 feet. A quiet submarine could sneak through a lot easier than a surface ship. Mohammad knew there was no way to avoid being seen. So, he sailed through the straits the same way dozens of other ships do every day. After all, he was doing nothing illegal, and treaties between three different countries and the United Nations guaranteed safe and unrestricted passage. He would just sail through. Once he cleared the straits, the Wind and the Light would move apart. This distance would increase as they proceeded west. Everything was going as planned.

Chapter Thirty-Eight

All four Iranian ships were now in the Atlantic Ocean. All were heading to the East Coast of the United States. Except for a minor inconvenience by some pirates, the plan had gone perfectly. Mohammad was reviewing the final plans when the ship's captain entered his room. "Sir, we are going to run into some bad weather. We can't go around it. We can get through, but we might have to slow down a little." Mohammad looked up, "We must keep on our schedule. The attacks must occur at the same time for maximum effect. Besides, once we attack, America will be on full alert. They will send every ship and plane they have. None of us will ever see home. I do not want this to turn into a suicide mission." Ther captain nodded and left the room. He closed the door behind him.

Mohammad shook his head and looked at the map of the East Coast of the United States. He calculated the time it would take for the ships to get there. He stared at the map and the three red circles on the three major port cities on that coast. They would not be port cities much longer. He would have to risk a quick satellite phone call to the other ships coming up from the south. He had to know that they were on time, or the mission would have to be adjusted. He got out his cell phone and dialed. The phone was answered on the second ring. "Status," he said. The answer came back immediately, "On schedule." Mohammad broke the connected and powered down the phone. No American spy agency would find him. He was partially right.

The National Security Agency picked up the call. What made it stand out was how short it was. Their computers timed the duration of calls. This call was so short that it stood out from all other calls made in the region. The conversation was not heard and only a general area from which the call was made could be determined. Still, it was a small piece of the puzzle. While satellites scanned the ocean for the ships. The same storm which threatened to delay the ships, also partial hid them from the eyes above. The storm also affected being observed by planes and ships. The four ships sailed on. They would be at their targets in less than a week. Hopefully, they would live through it. If not, then they would all be heroes and martyrs.

Jones had gotten very frustrated having to call General Harper every six hours, reporting nothing new. She was frustrated, as was Hernandez. She was sure the general was also. This day however would finally bring some results. A satellite caught two of the Iranian tanker ships going through the Straits of Gibraltar They were traveling west at almost 20 knots. They were about to enter a storm. This would greatly reduce the satellite's ability to monitor the ships. She called the Chairman immediately and passed the information on. General Harper advised her that the other two ships had been located. They were traveling northwest from Cape Town. He did not tell her the source of the information. She did not need to know the source, only the information.

Harper asked his chief intelligence officer to come to his office. The three star Army general arrived in 5 minutes. "Have you been monitoring this?" "Of course, Mr. Chairman," said the J-2. "Okay, then what is your best guess on what is going on?" The J-2 thought for a moment. He had the same problem of all military intelligence officer. The boss wants a guess based on limited or confusing information. Too cautious would not work. Being too sure could result in mission failure and the deaths of US forces. This was a common situation. One rarely has all the pieces of the puzzle.

"Well, we have four tankers; their cargo is unknown. Two came through the Straits and the other two came around Africa, and all seem to be heading this way also. There is no evidence of nuclear weapons, nor any other weapon of mass destruction. This guy Mohammad hates America. It is obvious from his coordinating the July 4th attacks. At the time, he was safe, back in Iran. Now I hear from our friends at Langley, that this guy is on one of the ships that left last and came through the Straits. If I was going to guess, they split up so as not to draw too much attention. I would also guess that they are all heading for the East Coast. They are not very fast and have no stealth capabilities. We should be able to see them before they get to shore. I will also guess the lawyers say they did nothing wrong yet, and we cannot intercept them in international waters." This plain talking general had worked his way up in the intelligence field. As a lieutenant, he had served as the intelligence officer for an airborne infantry battalion of the 82nd Airborne. With promotions came assignments to higher level units; brigade, division and corps. He served as the Army G-2 and now as the J-2 for the Joint Chiefs. He never sugar coated anything and told what he knew to be true and not what someone wanted to hear. He hated "Yes Man," they got people killed. He only hoped his bosses would believe him and use the information he provided wisely.

"Sounds reasonable," said Harper. "How are we going to determine their mission and stop it? We do not know where they are headed. We can not guard the entire East Coast." "Hopefully, we can get a better location as they approach the US. Then we can concentrate our forces to stop them, lawyers permitting." He smiled. So did Harper, but somewhat weakly. "Keep on it and let me know as soon as you can. I have the entire military coiled and ready to go, if we know where to go. Still do not know what they have planned, but I bet I will not like it. "I agree, boss." He turned and left for his office. The boss had good questions, now if he could only provide good answers.

Lieutenant General Phillip Thomas walked back to his office. As soon as he entered the room, he looked at his aide, "Full staff meeting in 15 minutes. Get everyone here." "Yes sir" snapped the aide and started dialing. In 13 minutes, the conference room was full from generals to sergeants. This was no time to stand on rank. "You all have the latest information. We know four ships are heading this direction. The boss needs to know what they are up to and where the attack will be. We are running out of time." There was a general modding of heads and a lot of conversations. After a few minutes, Harper called for answers. There weren't any. CW4 Eomas raised his hand. He had been an intelligence officer for decades but had spent most of his time in tactical and not strategic units. "Sir, it seems to me that we need a ship expert, no one here has that of experience." The room went quiet. Harper turned to his aide. "Run and I mean run to the CNO's office and ger me an experienced boat driver." A boat driver is a Surface Warfare Officer. A person with experience and a graduate of the Surface Warfare School. These were the people who ran and commanded our surface Navy. The aide got up and ran out of the room. They waited for his return.

Ten minutes later, a tall man in the Kakhi Navy uniform entered the room with the aide. His six rows of ribbons were displayed on his chest. His gold Surface Warfare Officer's badge was displayed about the ribbons.

"I am Navy Captain Hasting. I understand you have a few questions sir." Navy captains which were officer level six, the same as a full colonel in the other services. They did not wish to be confused with captains from the other services which were officer level three. It is a very big difference. General Thomas, not wishing to stand on ceremony or waste time, gave the captain what they knew. The general added, "The CIA feels that the use of chemical, bacteriological or nuclear weapons are not likely. This Mohammad is doing this operation on his own. At his own expense and with his own ships."

"Sir may I see the photos of the ships?" The satellite imagery, marked "Top Secret" were handed to the captain. His security clearance was well above Top Secret. The captain studied the photos for a few moments. "Does anyone have a magnifying glass?" asked Hastings. The general's aide opened a desk drawer and handed the lens to the captain. After a few moments of going back and forth between the pictures, the captain smiled. "Have you noticed that all four ships have hoisting cranes on their decks which could be used to raise or lower a boat? Three of the ships have boats on them, but not this one. So, three ships can raise or lower the boats. This last ship can recover the boats from the sea. These three boats are preparing to abandon their ships on purpose. Not as part of any rescue."

"Why would they do that?" asked one of the junior staff officers.

"Because the ships are going places the crew does not want to go. You say this Mohammad does not have access to weapons of mass destruction, but he does. These ships can carry about one million barrels of oil, depending on its size. The two ships that went around Africa can hold that much and maybe more. They would not have fit through the Suez Canal, so they took the long route. The other two ships were a little smaller and could fit through the canal. They might only hold 800,000 barrels of oil." The room went silent.

"So," said the Chairman, somewhere between 3 and 4 million barrels of oil are heading this way under the command of a man who hates Americans and has already conducted a terrorist attack on US soil."

"That would be a good evaluation," said Hastings.

"What is with the three smaller boats?" asked an Air Force Colonel. "They might be well made, but I doubt they could make it back to Iran."

"You are right," said Hastings. "But it is possible they could travel a moderate distance in the ocean and be picked up by one of the ships." "That is why the fourth ship does not have a boat."

"You are right, Mr. Chairman," said Hastings. "Abandoning their ships in the ocean does not assure whatever their mission is. If they plan to ram something with the ships, then why have an escape boat?" "The ships could be fitted with a GPS navigation system. Punch in the coordinates, engage the engines and get off the ship. It will go, at full speed, where it was sent."

"Oh my God, the destruction would be extreme, depending on what was hit," said one of the staff officers.

"I doubt the ships would be aimed at a beach somewhere. If it was me, I would aim them for our biggest ports and Naval bases," said Hastings.

Harper asked, "What would those targets be?"

Hastings looked the general directly and said, "New York, Norfolk, and Savannah. You take out the three biggest ports on the East Coast and throw in the largest American Naval Base for good measure. I understand he does not like our Navy much."

At this point, the Chairman sat down. "Does anyone have a better idea?" The room was very quiet. "Captain, I greatly appreciate your insight. I am sure I will be speaking to you very soon. You may return to your duties. The rest of you are also excused, I have a phone call to make."

General Harper picked up his secure phone and dialed the White House. It was answered on the first ring. "This is General Harper. I need to speak to the President." There was no need to identify himself, anyone answering that phone knew the people who were given that number. About two minutes later, the President came on the line. "General, what do you have for me?" Harper gave the President an update on all solid intelligence and then the estimate made by the Navy Captain. "By the time we know for sure, it may be too late to react. Mr. President, it could be accurate. Right now, we do not have a better guess. It would cause untold havoc and destruction. The fire department there would have a heck of a time trying to put out a million gallon fire, before it spread onto the docks and storage area. Those three ports would be closed for months, and that is if they could be rebuilt at all. We can get the Navy out of Norfolk, that would at least save the ships and the crews. We rely on Norfolk as it is the home base of the Atlantic fleet." The President told Harper he would get back to him in a few. He had a call to make. The President called the Director of the CIA. The President explained all that Harper had told him. "Well, what do you think?" The CIA Director said it sounded like a possible threat, but had no information that would confirm or refute the theory. The next call was to the DNI. He had input from other agencies. "The only thing he could add was that the four ships were now less than a day away from the coast and they seem to be getting closer to each other. At the current course and speed, they should be fairly close to each other in just a few hours. "I hope that helps, Mr. President." The President hung up and rubbed his face with both hands. Harry Truman was right, "The buck stops here."

Chapter Thirty-Nine

The President called Harper and gave him the green light to guard these ports. Save some forces for a reserve, if you are wrong. All military and civilian forces would be mobilized. The Coast Guard would be fully utilized. The president wished him luck. Harper thought, "if you are wrong." Thank you for the confidence. Harper called the Commandant of the Coast Guard. He read him in on the situation. Harper asked the Admiral what resources he could provide. The Admiral said he would get back to Harper in an hour. The other service chiefs were also alerted. They had two hours to come up with a plan to protect the coast and brief Harper. Time was running out.

Mohammad stood on the bridge of the Light. He was in position. The ship was over 100 miles off the South Carolina coast. The other ships were at their designated positions. The Prophet was 100 miles northeast of Savannah, Georgia. The Lion was 100 miles southeast of Norfolk, Virgina. The Wind was 100 miles south of the New York harbors. He would have to make a short call to each ship to assure they were ready for the attack, timing was important. He knew the ships would not crash into the piers at the exact same time, but it would be close enough. Each ship was loaded with as much fuel oil as it could carry. Each ship was also rigged with several explosive devices. One would go off if the ship impacted anything solid. The other device had a timer on it. Either way the ships would explode on their target, igniting about a million gallons of oil. The fire would be impossible to stop. It would spread and destroy docks and piers. Other ships would burn and the disaster would grow. It would cost him billions, wreck his shipping line, but he didn't care. After this he could relax and retire. His father would have been avenged. Someone else could worry about the company.

Once the ship's GPS had been programmed, the smaller boat would be lowered. As the crew of the tanker got onto the boat, the ship's captain would engage the engines and escape with his crew. They would travel at high speed to meet the Light. Once there, the crew and the boat would be winched aboard. Then the Light, at best possible speed, would travel to other pre-determined locations to pick up the next crew. Once all three crews were on board, the Light would return to Bandar Abbas. Mohammad would be satisfied and the three ship's crew would receive a huge bonus. It would be over. It would take hours for the three tankers to strike their targets. This would give them time to regroup and escape. No one would be looking for them, the Americans would have much bigger problems than a lone ship heading away from the United States in the middle of the night. The only problem was pickup up the three crews. The first two crews, Savannah and Norfolk would be fairly easy as they were close by. However, the Light would have to steam at full speed towards the crew on the Wind. Once the Wind was on its attack course, the crew would have to head towards the Light at full speed. The Light would do the same, closing the distance between them. It would be a race before they were discovered.

Mohammad took his satellite phone and called each ship. Each call would not last more than a few seconds. He did not want the Americans to even know he was in the area, let alone planning something. He had heard many stories about electronic listening to phone calls. Mohammad dialed the Prophet. "Ready?" "Yes" was the response. He broke the connection. This was repeated to the other two ships. In both cases, the answer was yes. He checked his watch. He would give the go signal in 8 minutes. The American would wake up on their holiday to fire, death and destruction.

Once again, the NSA picked up the very short phone calls from the middle of the ocean. They were unable to record the one word each caller said. They did however get a very general location for the calls. Had it not been for the alert from General Harper, they probably would have gone unnoticed. They would focus more assets on the area, just in case there was another call. Eight minutes later, there was another call. There were three calls, each less than five seconds in length. The problem was the NSA did not hear the go order and still could not pinpoint where the calls were made from. They could, however narrow the area down a little.

The NSA immediately sent the information to the Joint Chiefs' operations center. Here all information, from all sources was evaluated and analyzed. Jones and Hernandez had a direct line into the center.

With the intercepts from the NSA, the theory that there were three ships heading to attack the US East Coast got stronger. Even though it was the Labor Day weekend and many of the members of the military were on a three day pass, or as they called it, a training holiday. Harper called all the Service Chiefs and told them to screen the east coast for these ships. Keep something in reserve to attack these ships, if needed. Harper called Colonel Laskin.

"I have permission to deploy armed forces to protect our coast. At what point can we legally fire on these vessels?" asked Harper.

"Sir, if they fire on any of our forces or US property, deadly force would be legal," came the answer.

"Not good enough," said Harper. "We think they plan to ram these fuel laden ships into US post facilities and set them on fire."

"Sir, do you have any evidence?" Harper admitted that he did not. "Well then sir, you can't shoot, legally."

"How about when they enter our waters? Can we order them to stop?" "Yes sir, you can do that."

"Okay," said Harper, "If they don't stop, can we shoot then?"

"Sir, that is tricky. Suppose their radio is out or they do not understand?" "There are international signals that all vessels are supposed to understand," Haper said sensing his voice getting louder.

"Sir, legally, you would have to be able to prove their intent. Does that help sir?" asked Laskin.

Harper said, "No, it does not colonel. Thank you for your input." And hung up the phone. If it was easy, anyone could do it, was the old adage. Harper understood what it was saying.

Chapter Forty

All three tanker ships were now on automatic pilot. Their GPS devices were locked on their targets. Their engines were set for the maximum safe speed, assuring the engines would not be overloaded. They must reach their targets. The three crews had all safely gotten off their ships and were heading at full speed to their rendezvous with the Light and Mohammad. It would take many hours to reach their destination. They knew Mohammad would be coming for them and that would reduce the distance they had to travel. Once all three crews were on board, they would head home. They would be heroes and rich.

The alert flashed to all military bases along the East Coast. All ships and aircraft were to be ready to engage the tankers. Approval to open fire had been passed down to local flag rank commanders. There probably would not be time to request fire from the entire chain of command. Rules of Engagement was sent to every base and every major command. Doing the right thing under stress was what the military was all about. There would be not time to sit around and debate the finer points of the discussion. The lawyers, politicians and TV hosts could debate it, once the America was safe. Ships made their ammunition ready; aircraft were being fueled and armed. Whatever was about to happen would probably happen before the sun came up. A heck of a way to spend a 3 day weekend.

Captain Joshua Davis Moore was sitting in the cockpit of his F-35B Lightning II fighter. The plane was fueled and a variety of weapons were being mounted on his aircraft. On this mission, stealth was not important. Stopping the threat was. It had been six years since he graduated from Georgia Tech. After graduation, he looked for a purpose. His engineering degree did not get him a job he felt good about. Then he enlisted in the Marine Corps. He was offered to go to Officers Candidate School. It was the hardest thing he ever did. He was pushed to show him his new limits. Then on to infantry training and an assignment as a platoon leader. After 6 months as an infantry platoon leader, he put in for and was accepted to flight school. While not as physically demanding as OCS, the academics were unbelievable. He graduated and got his wings. Now there was more school to teach him the plane that would fly. He could not believe he was selected for the F-35B. The Marine variation of the F-35 which could stop in midair, move backwards and take off and land vertically. Once again, he had to study hard. College was so much easier than this.

Now he was assigned to Marine Corps Air Station Cherry Point, North Carolina. Only an eight hour drive from home in Atlanta. Life was good. Of course, sitting in a cockpit and not flying was not his idea of fun. He looked out of his cockpit and saw the other F-35B being armed. That was his wingman, or technically his wing woman was First Lieutenant Judy "Hook" Larsen. She had graduated first in her flight school class and learned the F-35B systems much faster than he did.

Both aircraft were loaded with two JDAM and cluster munitions in their internal bays. Since stealth was not required on this mission, a GAU-22/A and 220 rounds of ammunition was mounted under the aircraft. Only the Air Force version, the F-35A carried its gun internally. The planes were ready; the pilots were ready and now they waited.

The Air Force moved a squadron of E-3 Sentry aircraft from Tinker Air Force Base in Oklahoma to Pope Air Force Base in North Carolina. These aircraft, usually called AWACS, airborne warning and control systems, were unarmed versions of the old Boeing 707 commercial airliner. What made them obvious was the huge saucer shaped, thirty feet in diameter, revolving dome mounted over the aircraft. These planes were not designed for dog fighting or bombing missions. They were designed to see the battlefield and provide warning and communications to air and ground commanders. They could stay up for about eight hours and see hundreds of miles in all directions. They were the eyes in the sky. The Air Force now had one flying back and forth from North Carolina to New York. Another plane flew from North Carolina to Jacksonville, Florida. These two planes could see almost the entire East Coast. Anything at sea would be noticed. Another set of planes would take off for their patrol, before the first set can in for refueling and a short break for the crew.

Both Moore and Larsen had inspected their planes for the third time. They checked to make sure all ordinance was properly mounted.

Controls on the wings and tail were working properly. They also checked the engine nozzle. This model was unique. Most aircraft have their exhaust nozzles pointing to the rear. The F-35B also could pivot its nozzle downward, allowing it some amazing flight characteristics. This aircraft replaced the older Harrier aircraft which had similar characteristics. However, the F-35 was much stealthier and had far superior electronics than the older Harrier.

It seemed it was going to be another military "Hurry up and wait" drill. At about 0330 hours, an AWAC identified a lone tanker heading at full speed to the area of Savannah. The information was instantly transmitted to the Marine Base. Within a minute, a sergeant was running at full speed to the flight line. Moore and Larsen were standing outside their aircraft just talking and relaxing. They saw the sergeant running towards them. They knew. "Get up there, AWAC will vector you in. They have a lone tanker heading for Savannah." "They are attacking Georgia, my home state," thought Moore. He might have said it out loud as Larsen looked at him. Both pilots climbed into their plane. The highly trained ground crew helped them strap in. As the canopy closed, the flight crews backed away from the aircraft. No sense getting cooked by the jet exhaust. Bad for the career was the standard joke.

"This is Black Bird 1-6, request take off permission for 1-6 and 1-7," said Moore.

Instantly, a voice came over their headsets. "You are cleared for takeoff. Once airborne, contact Gold Eye 5," the tower gave the frequency for the AWACS.

Both F-35Bs powered up; they were already lined up on the runway. Moore looked at Larsen, gave her a thumbs up, and released the wheel brakes on the aircraft. The jet shot forward. As the plane lifted off the runaway, Moore gave the plane full power. Fuel conservation would not be a problem. He adjusted his radio to the AWACS frequency.

"Gold Eye 5, this is Black Bird 1-6, request vector to target. We are feet wet." Feet wet signified they were over water. In this case, the Atlantic Ocean.

"This is Gold Eye 5, target traveling at 22 knots on a course of 270. They are heading directly for the harbor in Savannah, if they do not change course. The ship has no electronic signature." This means the ship had no radar or radio emissions. She was totally dark.

"Roger," said Moore. He knew Larsen had heard the same information.

The two F-35Bs changed courses to intercept the tanker. They would have a visual on the tanker in less than ten minutes. "What kind of ordinance do you think we should use?" asked Larsen. "Let's wait and see what is going on. We have to make sure this is the right target." At their speed, we have a few minutes to check them out. As they approached the ship, both aircraft slowed and dropped in altitude. Moore could see the ship. Gold Eye, as usual, put them exactly on the right vector. The ship was still traveling at 22 knots and on a direct course for Savannah.

"Stay at 5,000 feet and watch out for missiles. I am going to take a closer look," said Moore.

"Watch yourself, if they have missiles, you will be a sitting duck," said Larsen.

"I know, but before a blow up a civilian ship, I want to make sure." Moore slowed his plane even further and dropped down to 100 feet about sea level. He approached the side from the stern. He saw no lights of any kind. He slowed his plane almost to walking speed. There was no one on the deck. He paused midair for a moment and looked at the bridge. There was always someone on the bridge. But not in this case. There were no signs of life, no one piloting the ship. He had never heard of a ship this size with an auto pilot, but now it looks like he had one.

"Buzz, this is Hook. We will be within the 12-mile limit in a minute or so."

Moore answered, "I know. No one appears to be on board, even the bridge is blacked out and enemy."

"Okay," said Hook. "Move away from it and let's blow it up."

"Negative Hook" came back the response. "If we blow her up, there will be oil everywhere. It will drift onto the shore with these currents. The entire Savannah area will be polluted for years. I am not doing that."

"So, we use smaller munitions and set it ablaze."

"Can't do that either," said Moore. "If we burn it, we get toxic smoke. I am not sure where it will go. What doesn't burn will populate the harbor area. Again, not a great result." The radios were silent for a few seconds. "I am going to try to stop the ship."

"Buzz, you are crazy. You are not a SEAL. You can't just eject, land on the ship and take it over. That is sheer madness"

"You are absolutely right." Moore acknowledged. "Here is what I want you to do. Climb to Angels 3 and wait. I have an idea, maybe a crazy one but still an idea. If it doesn't work, I will move away from the ship and you pound it with high explosives and incendiaries. We will burn it and hope little oil and toxic wastes makes it to shore." He thought that the ocean would die around the flaming ship.

Moore pulled alongside the huge ship. He stopped his plane in midair. He knew he could only hold this position for a few moments. He turned the fighter to face the bridge of the ship. He also knew he only had 220 rounds of ammunition to use in this plane. The idea of a toxic beach and foul air over his home state was not acceptable. He pointed the nose of his plane directly at the bridge of the ship. He selected guns and fired a short burst. The cannon roared. Moore could feel the vibration throughout the plane. The wheel house exploded. At this range, Moore could not miss. The structure shattered. Pieces were flying everywhere. The ship continued on its course. Moore repositioned the jet and fired another burst. The remainder of the bridge seemed to explode. Small fires could be seen where the bridge once was. The ship continued on. Moore looked at the counter. He had 180 rounds left in the gun.

Hook came on the air, "I can see the lights of Savannah in the distance. Whatever you are going to do, do it fast." Moore thought for a moment. He gained a little altitude, pointed the plane's nose down at the bridge and fired a longer burst. He reasoned the electronics controlling the ship would be on the floor and not on the side of the structure. The structure which was no longer there. He let off a longer burst. The deck which supported the bridge took the fury of the shells. Part flew in all directions. More fires were seen. The ship sailed on. Moore had 140 shells left. He might as well use them up. His brilliant idea had failed. His beloved state would be polluted, people would become sick, commerce would stop.

"No," he yelled to himself. He pushed the throttles forward and gained altitude. "Hook, back away now!" he screamed into the radio. He was at 5.000 feet. He turned the jet and pointed it straight down at the bridge. His plane dove, picking up speed.

"Buzz, don't," screamed Larsen, fearing a suicide mission. At about 2,000 feet, Moore could see the bridge of the tanker directly in front of him. He pulled the trigger and the cannon came to life. The 25mm shells rained down on the ship. The entire bridge was gone. Shells cut through the steel. Nothing in the bridge area could survive the destruction. Not even the electronic auto pilot. Moore grabbed the stick and pulled hard. The nose of the jet started to lift. The G-forces were worse than anything he had ever experienced. Everything became grey, his field of vision rapidly shrunk. He could barely see anything. Somehow the nose of the plane became level. Moore eased off on the stick and his vision started to return.

"Buzz, you stupid son of bitch, you did it," screamed Larsen. Moore was still clearing his head, but the words sounded good. He leveled off the aircraft and flew like a normal person. While there were fires on the ship where the bridge use to be, the ship had come to a stop. Without its electronic guidance, the ship had no idea what to do.

"I have got to land this plane, the Gs kicked my ass," said Moore. "Call the base and ask the Navy to come out here and tow this ship in." The two F-35s returned home in triumph. Savannah was safe.

Chapter Forty-One

While Marine aviation was safeguarding Savannah, another ship, the Lion, was traveling at full speed to Norfolk, Virginia. The Port of Virginia is a huge port. It covered almost 1,900 acres. It serves both numerous cargo ships and cruise ships. American's largest naval base was also located nearby. This base was home to thousands of military personnel, civilian workers and the families of these workers. It had more activity than many US cities. The Navy base was home to over six dozen ships and well over 100 aircraft of varying types. It is a target that would rank on the top of any enemy's list. Unfortunately, most of the ships assigned there were either patrolling the Atlantic or on temporary duty in the Middle East. Sea power in the Middle East was critical. There were of course Navy ships in Norfolk. Many of them were undergoing repairs or upgrade and could not immediately put out to sea, no matter how important the mission. After long sea voyages, many of the crew members were allowed to take time off to see their families. Being at sea from six months can really strain family life. A three day Labor Day weekend is ideal for families to be together. So, when one of the AWACS picked a tanker ship heading at full speed directly at the port area, the Naval base was called. There were several warships in port. Before they could get underway, their crews would have to be recalled and munitions loaded. Doing repair work with a storage area full of explosives was not a good idea. Naval operations told the AWACS the expected response time. This would not be good enough. The ships in the Atlantic were also notified. They were midway between Norfolk and the Straits of Gibraltar looking of the last two ships to leave Iran. There were two destroyers which were much closer to the American Coast than the rest of the screening force. They immediately set course for Norfolk. At top speed, they would be too late.

The AWACS called the Coast Guard station in Portsmouth, Virginia. True to their motto, "Semper Paratus," Always Ready, the Coast Guard duty officer told the AWACS that he would have a cutter moving in less than fifteen minutes. The alert siren was sounded and a stream of men and women streamed out of buildings on onto the Cutter Grizzly. The voice of the duty officer boomed over load speakers, "Incoming terrorist ship, this is not a drill." Commander Scott Warner ran to the bridge. The chief of the boat, the COB was already there. The COB was the senior enlisted member of the crew. "COB, how long before we can sail?" "Less than 5, Skipper. We are taking a lot of short cuts," Commander Warner got on the radio and asked operations what was going on. "There is an Iranian flagged oil tanker, she is blacked out and on some kind of autopilot. Apparently, there is no one on board. She is heading directly into the harbor. Sounds like a kamikaze mission. Slow them down or stop them at all costs. She is fully loaded with old. We will either have a huge fire and explosion or a huge natural environmental disaster, or both. I have a maritime security response team spinning up. A Seahawk will get them out there. However, it will take a while to get them here and loaded up. There are also two Navy destroyers trying to catch up. AWACS says they will not make it here in time, go get her Scott." Warner acknowledged the information and was given a vector to intercept the ship. At maximum speed, the cutter would catch up to the tanker when she was well inside US waters. This would be close.

"COB, get us moving now," ordered Warner. Even as he said that he could see that the lines which held the Cutter to the pier had been released. The twin turbo charged V-18 diesel engines were running. The ship was moving away from the pier. "This is a hot mission. Give it everything you got. Try not to wreck my ship." The crew had heard the communications between their captain and operations. A ship's commanding officer was referred to as captain, even if that was not his actual rank. They knew what was at stake. They smiled at his last comment. They knew the ship's main purpose was to protect life and property. The ship cleared the harbor and proceeded on the course provided by the AWACS.

At 270 feet long, the ship was less than a third the size of the tanker and about half the size of a Navy destroyer. Still, she was armed with two heavy machine guns and a main deck gun. Her job was to stop the tanker, not sink her. The 100 people of the crew worked like a Swiss watch. Total team work. Without this team work, their mission would fail. The SPS-78 search radar was activated and monitored for their target or any other ships in the area. Collisions at sea were frowned upon. They were career enders, even without injuries. The crew was ready; the ship was ready. Now if they could only find the tanker.

"Skipper, we're closing on the ship. We have her on radar. Now what?" asked the XO.

Lieutenant Commander Harkness had just been promoted to Lieutenant Commander. This would be his first assignment at his current rank. He was overjoyed to be the second in command of a Cutter. He thought he would get a staff job writing reports or ordering supplies. Of course, his training had never covered stopped a ship, at night, loaded with explosive fuel, with no time to plan. He was up for a challenge.

Warner considered his opinions. He could not fire on the ship, trying to disable her. He would either set it on fire or sink her. Both would cause a huge environmental disaster. This would be better than letting it crash into the docks in Virginia. Let's hold off on that opinion. He thought about trying to damage the rudder. Then he would have no idea where the ship would go. Maybe he could spread cables in front of her and hope to foul her screws. The screws were the propeller like objects which pushed the ship. That was not going to work either. He would need a lot of cable and a way of holding it in from of the tanker until she ran over it. Nope, not that way. "Get the helio ready," said Warner, "I have an idea." "Aye aye" came the answer.

"XO, here is the plan. We are not waiting for the security response team. There is not supposed to be anyone on board the ship. So, no one should get in my way. I am going to have the helio drop me on the deck. I will find and disable this autopilot device. Once done, the tanker can be sailed to where ever command wants it docked. Security can disarm any explosives on board. Once I get it stopped, the helio can pick me up and return me to the Grizzly. We will wait for everyone else to get here and turn the tanker over to them."

The XO was stunned. "Sir, with respect, do you know how to do that?"

"Can't be too hard, the Iranian sailors turned it on." There was a moment of silence.

The XO asked, "What if you can't deactivate the device?"

"Then, if the tanker gets within six miles of the shore, you will open fire on the tanker and stop her. Under no circumstance will you let it get inside six miles of the coast." "Sir, what about you?"

"If I can, I will jump into the sea and swim. I don't think my chances would be very good. Look at the bright side, you just made Lieutenant Commander and you will be in command of a Cutter." The XO did not think that was very funny. "I am sure I will be okay. Anyone haver a better idea?"

The helicopter, an MH-65 Dolphin, was rolled out of its hangar on the rear of the ship. Its rotor blades were extended.

Lieutenant Lisa George was doing an abbreviated preflight check, as Commander Warner, dressed in a bright orange safety suit approached. The blades were starting to turn as Warner yelled over the noise, "Put me down as close as you can to the bridge. Once I disconnect from the hoist, back away. If I set this thing off, I do not want you and the bird caught in the fireball." She nodded. Warner went to the hoist on the starboard side of the helicopter and snapped the link to the straps on his safety suit. Once done, he got in the helicopter. It would be a very short flight.

The helio lifted off the deck and headed for the tanker. The Grizzly continued to parallel the tanker and matched its speed. They were separated by about a mile of ocean. The ship's crew continued to look for the Navy or the Maritime Unit. The radar showed nothing. They were notified that the Maritime Unit was about to lift off from their base in Virginia and would be heading their way. The crew watched Lieutenant George hover the helio directly over the bridge. She moved a little to the left and Commander Warner started to come down on the hoist. His feet hit a walkway just a few feet from the bridge. Warner told himself to thank George for great flying. He was lowered down with almost no swinging. Swinging or spinning was not uncommon. Warner released the hoist cable and waved at George. She moved away from him. She stopped and hovered about half way between the tanker and the Grizzly. She was ready to pick up her commanding officer the second he requested it.

Warner went to the door to the bridge. It was unlocked. He opened the door and walked onto the bridge. It looked like the bridges he had seen various times. Nothing out of the ordinary, except for a large silver colored metal box on the floor near the ship's control panel. This had to be it. He knelt down next to the box. It had a series of lights on the front of the box. Warner examined the box for a door to access the interior of the box. There were none. Just then Warner heard his XO on his radio. Warner was told that the Iranian boat would enter the six mile limit within 2 minutes. Did Warner want to cancel his order to fire on the tanker? "Negative, follow the orders. Norfolk must be protected." Warner went to work on the metal box. He could find no way to open the box. He pulled out a large knife and tried to punch a hole through the metal. The knife was useless. Warner heard his XO telling him he had one minute before the XO would open fire. Warner wished he could say goodbye to his wife and kids. This was not to be. Warner stared at the control panel on the face of the box. There were five green lit rocker switches and one red lit rocker switch. It could not be that easy. Thirty seconds. Oh well, might as well try. "I love you, my family," he said out loud and pushed the red rocker switch.

There was an immediate change in the sound of the ship. Warner could feel the ship slowing. Numerous lights on the ship's control panel went out. All the lights on the silver box went out. The ship slowed further. "Great job, Sir!" came the XO's voice over the radio. The ship stopped; its engines were off. Warner stood up. His knees were weak. He walked outside of the bridge. The fresh sea air felt good. He saw the helio coming for him. George placed the hook about three from Warner. Warner almost reached out to grab the hook. He remembered the static charge which could be built up in the cable. Warner picked up a boat hook. He held the wooden handle and used the metal hook to pull the cable to him. There had been a small spark when the metal hook made contact. In the daylight, he would not have seen the spark. He hooked the cable to his safety suit. George lifted him up and returned him to the Grizzly. He unhooked and walked back to the bridge. As he walked in, the XO yelled, "Captain on the bridge." This was followed by a round of applause and a lot of yelling. Warner, exhausted, sat in his chair. He needed to rest. "Sir," said the COB, "Maritime Security one minute out."

"Thank them, tell them the tanker is dead in the water. She is all theirs. The COB passed the message. The COB approached Warner. "Sir, that was the bravest thing I have even seen. Words fail me."

"XO, I will be in my cabin. Stay here until the Navy gets here and the Maritime unit does not need us. Then on to Norfolk." Warner went to his cabin and laid down. He was asleep in seconds.

Chapter Forty-Two

Commander Robert Cox was the commanding officer of the U.S.S Tulsa. A Los Angeles class U.S. Navy attack submarine. The L.A. Class were getting old and being replaced by the newer Virginia Class sub. He had been the commanding officer for fourteen months. He knew he was coming to the end of his time on the sub. This is where he was supposed to be. He knew he might get an assignment on high Navy or Joint Staff. This would help his chances of getting promoted. He would miss being at sea.

The sub was about 362 feet long but only about 33 feet wide. Over 120 people worked on this boat. All submarines were boats, not ships. Its nuclear engine would not need fuel in his lifetime. They could basically cruise forever. Of course, the crew would need rest and a resupply of food would be needed every now and then. Their place was under the waves. Unlike World War II, these boat's interior was clean and the air was also. Modern subs had both torpedoes and missiles. They did not have to get close to their target, unlike the WWII brothers. This class of sub was interesting. It could travel faster underwater than on the surface. A lot of folks had problems understanding that. Afterall, it was easier to go through the air than the water.

The boat had just finished a 90-day patrol. They patrolled an area between Greenland and Iceland, and the area just to the south. Their mission was to monitor naval traffic, especially Russian ships and subs. They would follow the Russian vessels and relay their activities to the next higher command. It was a game of cat and mouse. The American subs usually won. Now the patrol was over. They were headed back to the New London Navy Base in Groton, Connecticut. They were passing Nova Scotia. Once at their home base, the crew would be able to take leave, see family and friends and blow off steam. Cox would have a week's worth of paperwork. Then he would probably be relieved and given a desk job. Such is the way things worked. His superiors would see this as giving him a career enhancing job. They were doing him a favor. One day, he would hope to be promoted and be in charge of a squadron of subs. This was his ultimate Navy goal.

His XO approached him. "Skipper, we just got a flash message from COMSUBLANT, the commander of all U.S. subs in the Atlantic. This three star admiral was Cox's overall boss. His messages were read immediately. Cox started to read the message and then stopped. "COB, you need to see this." Command Master Chief Edwards had more time in subs than anyone else in the boat. He had worked every type of assignment from navigation, to weapons, the reactor and communications. If it was on this boat, he knew it. The three men read the message. It detailed about the upcoming terrorist attacks on the east coast. It talked about the 3 or 4 tankers approaching the coast. The Tulsa was to proceed at maximum speed to protect the New York – New Jersey area. Once they identified the tanker, they were to stop it and try not to pollute the ocean or the air. The message did not give instructions on how to do that. It was very difficult to reason with an unmanned ship three times their size.

The Port of New York – New Jersey was the largest and busiest port on the East Coast of the United States. Cargo from all over the world was arriving daily. Likewise, ships left the port daily and travelled the oceans bring every kind of cargo. This port was essential for global trade and the American economy. Millions of tons of products passed through the port annually. The effect of an exploding tanker in the port was beyond imagination. What could be imagined would give anyone nightmares.

"I want a course set for New York City, maximum speed. Push the engines. This old girl still has fight in her. Get communications with COMSUBLANT. Any information about this would be appreciated. Those who can, get some rest. We will be a battle stations soon, "ordered Cox. The boat changed course and the crew could feel the increase in speed. The next few hours could change American.

Mohammad was on the bridge of the Light. He had picked up the first two crews and was now heading to get the last crew. Once they were on board, the ship would head directly to Bandar Abbas. He was in international waters and should be safe from an attack by the Americans. After all, he had done nothing wrong. He just picked up some employees, in international waters and was taking them home. They had abandoned their ship due to "mechanical problems." The three ships would be on course. It would be a few more hours before they struck their targets. By that time, he hoped to be far away from the American Coast. He would monitor the radio for any news. Surely, there would be news right away after the ships detonated against the docks and piers. He could sail home happy.

The Wind had been put on autopilot, and the crew had gotten off quickly. They did not want to be near this floating bomb if the Americans discovered them. They would travel for several hours and hope that their navigation was accurate. They had limited food and water on this small boat. Finding the Light was their sole purpose now. The Wind would do what it was supposed to do.

The Tulsa had passed New Shoreham and was approaching Montauk Point at the eastern point of Long Island, New York. The engines were still going strong, although one of the reactor mechanics expressed concern about overheating the engine. The temperature was still in the green but was only the slightest bit from entering the yellow on the safety dial. They were running shallow in the water. They needed to be able to communicate with anyone who was trying to reach them.

"Tulsa, this is Gold Eye 2," came over the radio; it was an Air Force AWACS.

"This is Tulsa actual, go ahead," said Cox.

The AWACS advised that there were two unknown tankers and some sort of small boat in the area east of Atlantic City. One ship was heading towards New York City. The small boat had jointed up with the other tanker. That tanker then turned east and was proceeding away from the US coast. There was no sign of the small boat on radar. There had been no electronic emissions from any of the vessels.

"Can you give me the coordinates, direction, and speed of the boat heading for New York?" asked Cox. The AWACS did. "Thank you," said Cox. "Do you have any aircraft in the area that can engage the tanker? "Negative" came the reply from the AWACS. "What was the Air Force doing?" thought Cox. He knew there were no fighter units stationed near New York. The nearest Navy carrier was hours away, if they had aircraft they could launch. He knew the storm was still raging in the Eastern Atlantic.

Cox gave the new intercept course to the navigation officer. The boat changed course.

"What speed, Sir?" asked the helmsman. "Give it all she's got. We have to catch that ship." "Engineering" he said over the MC-1, push her into the red." "Boatswain mate, sound general quarters, this is not a drill." The klaxon sounded throughout the ship. Every person on the boat responded immediately. They had practiced this many times. Everyone knew where they were supposed to be and got there on a dead run. No one is off duty during general quarters.

Each division of the boat reported in that they were at battle stations. Missiles were being warmed up and torpedoes were being loaded into the torpedo tubes. Normally this was done quietly to prevent the enemy from knowing that they were there. This time, it did not matter. The boat was ready for war.

The AWACS continued to update the sub with the location of the tanker. The sub made corrections to close with the tanker. The AWACS also advised that the other tanker was still moving directly away from the coast.

The S6G nuclear reactor continued to push the sub at the maximum safe speed. Even so, things were heating up. The two steam turbines spun at speeds that were not recommended. The East Coast had to be protected, even at the cost of this boat.

"Do we have them on radar yet?"

"No, Sir, should have them very shortly."

"Based on the information provided by the AWACS, the tanker will be within 10 miles of the coast in a minute or so," said the XO. "We are closing, but it will be very close. It only takes a few minutes for her to get within six miles." "I want an audible count every thirty seconds. I want to know how far they are from the six mile limit and how far we are from them. Weapons officer, prepare two Harpoon missiles for immediately launch. We should know their exact location in a moment or so. I want those birds ready to fly." "Aye aye," answered the weapons officer, his fingers were pressing buttons and flipping switches. Several red lights turned green.

"Sir, surface contact, heading 290, speed 19 knots."

"Gold Eye 2, this is Tulsa actual. We have a surface contact," Cox read out the exact coordinates of the contact. "Can you confirm that is my target? We have missiles ready." Cox waited for what seemed to be minutes. It was in fact about eight seconds.

"Tulsa actual, Gold Eye 2, confirmed that is your target. I say again, that is your target.

It is now about 7 miles from the harbor." Cox voice got louder, "Weapons Officer lock in on that ship. "Already done" was the instant response. "Fire both harpoons" commanded Cox. The weapons officer, a young lieutenant, who had never fired a shot in anger, depressed two buttons and the Harpoon missiles launched from the bow torpedo tubes. Both of the fifteen foot long missiles broke the surface of the water, extended their fins and accelerated. At a speed of over 500 mph, the Harpoons and their 500 pound warheads would reach their target in just a few minutes. The Tulsa continued to close on the tanker.

The missiles streaked through the night sky. Two bright objects flew only a few feet above the ocean. The weapons officer counted down the time until impact. There were two loud explosions that no one heard. Both missiles had slammed into the bow of the ship.

The ship slowed dramatically from 18 knots to 2 knots. The missing bow provided tremendous resistance against the ocean. Fire broke out immediately. The fire spread throughout the ship. There were numerous smaller explosions due to the fire detonating various container of fuel. The Tulsa now rapidly closed on the tanker.

"Slow to 2/3, raise the periscope. The boat slowed and the strain on the turbines dropped well into the safety levels. The periscope was raised. Unlike the periscopes of early subs, modern periscopes do not use reflective mirrors in a metal tube. Modern periscopes are electronic cameras that work day or night and have electronic zoom lens. It is important to know what you are shooting at. Cox could see the massive fire in the distance.

"Bring us to within 5,000 yards. Reduce speed to 1/3." Said Cox. The XO and the COB also looked at the burning ship.

The XO said, "Skipper, this ship could burn for hours or days. It is a threat to other ships in the area. It could explode at any time." "What do you suggest XO?" "Sir, we need to sink her, end this. I recommend a torpedo."

Cox considered this and agreed. "Okay XO, it is your show, sink her."

The XO grinned. He had fired practice torpedoes before, but never a live one. One packed with almost 650 pounds of high explosives. Admittedly, the target was just about stationery and incapable of fighting back or even maneuvering to avoid the nineteen foot long torpedo. The XO gave the commands to the weapons officer who readied the torpedo. The weapon had already been loaded into a tube located by the bow of the boat. For this weapon, the range of 5,000 yards was almost too easy of a shot. The weapon has a range in miles, not yards. At a speed of about 70 mph, it would hit in just a few seconds. The XO thought of the old expression about shooting fish in a barrel. Then he remembered another saying, "It isn't over until it is over." The weapons officer advised he was ready to fire. "Fire one," said the XO. The 3,500 pound weapon blasted out of the tube. The XO knew this torpedo could guide itself or be guided from the sub. At this distance, it was an easy shot.

In less than a minute, the torpedo was directly underneath the tanker. World War Two torpedoes exploded on contact, blowing a hole in the ship. Modern torpedoes were different. Once it was directly under the target ship, it exploded with such force as to lift the ship up. The blast breaking the ship's hull. On some ships, the blast could be seen to actually lift the target out of the water. The XO watched through the periscope. The explosion rocked the tanker. For a moment the massive fireball obscured the ship from view. Then what was left of the tanker started to sink. Fire was everywhere, Fron the bow to the stern and on the water around the ship, The XO was glad that no one was on the ship. It would have been a living hell. The XO gave the periscope to Cox, who let the COB look also. The tanker went under, flames still on her deck. Even after the ship sunk, burning oil could be seen on the water. The threat to the New York – New Jersey waterfront was over. A round of applause went up on the Tulsa. They had actually sunk a ship and prevented a disaster. They would rely a report to COMSUBLANT and head for home. There would be a lot of paperwork to do. The crew would be given the leave they both needed and earned. Cox though at least his last voyage went off with a bang. The sub continued on to home. The Coast Guard would survey the wreckage and the oil spill. The cleanup would be massive, but the East Coast would be spared the fire and destruction planned.

Chapter Forty-Three

They sat around the large table. They were all waiting for the President. The National Security Advisor, the Attorney General, all the Joint Chiefs, the FBI and DHS directors. The Vice President stood near the head of the table. He was reading the summary report. The details would be reviewed when the President arrived. The DNI had a stack of papers in front of him. He was reviewing them. The CIA Director was seated next to the man who, in theory, was her boss. She had worked her way up in the Agency. When the last director retired, she was the ideal candidate. All were prepared for any question the President might ask. That was the trick for any staff officer. Quess what possible question they could be asked and have the answer ready. Saying, "I'll get back to you on that," is not the way to keep your job.

Exactly at 10 A.M., the President, some staffers, and his military aide walked into the room. Everyone stood. The President went to the head of the table. As he sat down, he waved for everyone else to sit. "Okay, I want a down and dirty summary of what has happened in the 60 days or so. No fancy slides. No big words. Not sugar coating." Several people at the table removed some files and Power Point slides from the table. Briefing with slides was a government standard. Some folks spent more time making the slides than was needed to present the information.

"I want to start this meeting by commending the Attorney General. Thanks to his actions, the 4th of July attack was prepared for and many, many lives were saved. FBI Director, do you have the numbers on the attacks?" The President like to use titles, rather than names at these meetings to keep them formal. He could, of course, use either. The FBI Director shuffled some papers, looking of the numbers. "Yes, Mr. President, right here. There was a total of 51 attacks. One in each state capitol and one outside the Capitol Building. Thirty one terrorists died. Twenty two were captured." The President interrupted, "That adds up to fifty-three." "Yes, Sir," continued the FBI Director, there were three terrorists on the DC attack. "Oh yes, I'm sorry. Those Marshals did an outstanding job of anticipating and stopping that attack. Has that Marshal which jumped on the grenade recovered?" The FBI Director and the AG looked at each other. The AG replied, "I'll have to get back to you on that" "Damn it man, that Marshal laid it all on the line, we should keep better track of him," said the President. The room got very quiet. The AG nodded his head. "There were 351 people killed and another 1246 injured. Some very seriously, they remain in the hospital. There were of course tens of thousands of dollars of damage." The President shook his head. "I wonder what would have happened if we did not get advanced warning on this?"

"Harper," said the President, "What about the attacks on our ports?"

General Harper knew that question was coming. "Mr. President, all three attacks were stopped. In two cases, the ships were stopped without major destruction of the ship. In the case of the ship that was within 6 miles of New York City, a Navy sub destroyed it using Harpoon missiles and a torpedo. Fire consumed most of the oil. The Coast Guard responded to the scene and will supervise the cleanup. There is no threat to navigation." "How were the other two stopped?" asked the President?

"Sir, the ship heading for Savannah was stopped when a Marine pilot dove at the ship and shot out the mechanism controlling the ship. It was some pretty fancy flying." The Commandant of the Marine Corps smiled and nodded his head. He was obviously proud of his pilot. "In regards to the ship heading for Norfolk, a Coast Guard officer was lowered onto the deck of the moving ship. He disabled the control mechanism on his own. I would like to point out that this officer gave the order to destroy the ship and himself if it got within the six mile limit. He cut it very, very close."

The President smiled. "That was outstanding work, really outstanding. I am proud of these fine people who averted major disasters across the East Coast. I want the heads of the service which are over these heroes, to put them in for awards. Whichever you think is appropriate. I do not want the paperwork lost in the shuffle. Write it up and bring it to me directly. These folks need recognition now and not in a few years." There was a general, "Yes Sir" from around the table. "I also want to speak to Marshal Tower. AG set up an appointment. "Of course, Mr. President."

"Now," asked the President, "What do we do about this character who caused the problems?" The DNI answered. "Sir, his name is Mohammad Abu al-Fadi. He is now back at home in Bandar Abbas, Iran. He is a wealthy shipping magnate. His father was killed by the Navy earlier this year. He was transporting weapons from Oman when challenged by the Navy destroyer. Several people on the deck opened fire with automatic weapons and RPGs. They struck the destroyer repeatedly. The destroyer fired back destroying the bridge of the ship and killed this guy's father and numerous people who fired at the destroyer. A complete investigation was conducted and the ship's captain was deemed to have taken appropriate action to safeguard his ship and crew. This event, we believe, is the spark that started all this. Prior to this event he was not on our radar. He was not political." "CNO," said the President looking at the four star admiral. If you believe the destroyer captain deserves an award. Please forward that to me directly." "Yes, Sir," said the Admiral. "Back to my question. What do we do with this guy?"

"Mr. President, we have several options," said the CIA Director. "First option, we just let it go. He was not on any of the ships that attacked us, nor was he part of the July 4th attack. He did however direct, led and coordinate these attacks. I strongly recommend against this option." Everyone nodded to agree. Option two. We get an internation warrant for his arrest and present it to the internation court. We can not present it to Iran as we do not have formal relations with them. They would probably ignore it anyway. If he did turn himself in, we would have to have a public trail, let his lawyers talk for hours about US aggression in the Middle East and have a sounding board for terrorism. The news media would eat it up. I strongly recommend against this option. Option three, is a capture mission. This would involve US military to covertly enter Iran and kidnap this guy. Then have to sneak him out of the country, this would put our forces at risk. We would be invading a sovereign country. The Iranians could and would open fire on our forces. Taking a live prisoner out would be very hazardous. This is not a good option." The Attorney General moved about in his seat. Having the military go into a foreign country and kidnap someone had been done before. He just didn't like it. "The fourth option is for US forces to covertly go to Bandar Abbas and kill him." Everyone went quiet and stared. This type of operation may have been done before, but the President always had deniability. To say this in an open session would be the President signing the death warrant of a foreign citizen, in a foreign country, without any legal proceedings.

"Would the Director of the CIA, the DNI, General Harper, and the Attorney General please remain. The rest of you are excused and thank you," said the President. The other members of the group left the room. They knew what was going to be discussed.

"Gentleman, I am preferring option four. I do not want to give this mass murder a chance to explain his position, use our legal system against us. I doubt the International Court will try him. I know Iran will not release him to us. He might sit in GITMO for years waiting for a trail. I do not want him to be a celebrity."

"Mr. President, I have to object. We are a nation of laws. We do not just execute people suspected of crimes," said the AG. "Which option do you want to use? Let me ask this, do you have any doubt he ordered the attacks on July 4th? Do you have any doubt he tried to use a weapon of mass destruction on three major US port cities? What would be the penalty for these crimes?" asked the President. The AG was stunned. A few minutes ago, the President was praising him in front of the entire room. Now he felt as if he was on the outside, looking in.

"Mr. President, I have no doubt that this Mohammad charter is guilty of these charges. If convicted, he would surely be put to death. I would agree with that sentence. Fighting terrorist have resulted in Supreme Court decisions which support a terrorist rights. I am sure you remember the case of Boumediene Verus President Bush in 2008. The Supreme Court said terrorists in US custody had the same rights as any American citizen." The President responded, "You are of course right. I remember that court case. I remember teams of soldiers and civilians going over classified documents to declassify those documents so the terrorist and his lawyer would not get classified material but there had to be enough unclassified documents to show a federal judge probably cause to hold the SOB." The President pulsed.

"I think the key words here are in US custody. I do not want him in custody. I want him dead." Those words shocked the room.

"The hundreds of dead innocent Americans, the thousands of injured Americans, their pain and healing process. The damage that would have happened if our brave men and women had not engaged those tankers before they rammed their way into our three biggest East Coast ports. I can live with this decision. Can you live with the media circus over the years of his trail. Even if convicted, there would be appeal after appeal. He could probably write a book or be interviewed for TV. Do you want this? Give me a better option!" The room went quiet. Only the sound of the air conditioner could be heard. The AG thought for a minute or two. Everyone else just waited. Finally, the AG said, "I do not like it, but I do not have a better idea." "Thank you for your honesty and ethics," said the President. "I always want to hear your opinions and get your input. I treasure your integrity. However, in this case I am going with option 4. I alone will take the heat if this blows up in our faces. General," the President said "you have my orders to come up with a reasonably safe plan to carry out this mission. I will expect a draft overview within 72 hours. Keep the circle of planners small. This must be a closely guarded secret for a variety of reasons." "Yes Mr. President," replied General Harper.

Harper returned to the White House in two days. "Mr. President, I think we have a working plan. Apparently CENTCOM had already tasked SOCCENT to plan for this. They were never given the go signal and they were getting intelligence from the CIA on the layout of this guy's house, his security, etc. They will insert a SEAL team by submarine to within a mile of the coast. The SEALs will exit the submerged sub, swim to the shore, accomplish the mission and leave the way they came. In and out, trying not to draw any attention to themselves. I do not think the Iranians would be very nice to an American military invasion trying to kill one of their local well connected citizens." "How long before thcy would be ready to go?" asked the President. "Their planning phase is complete, the have the equipment needed. Maybe a day or two to get a submarine and get it in place." Said Harper. "Do it," said the President. "Yes, Sir." answered Harper. He left the Oval Office and head back to his office at the Pentagon. He had a phone call to make.

About an hour later, the President's phone buzzed. "Mr. President, Marshal Tower is here," said the female voice. "Send him in."

"You wanted to see me, Mr. President."

"Yes, please have a seat. First, I want to know how that injured Marshal is doing. Carpenter, I believe."

"Yes, sir. He is out of the hospital but it will be a long, slow recovery. He goes to physical therapy three times a week. He is a fighter."

The President smiled. "Tell him if he needs anything, just ask. His bravery saved many lives. Tell him his job is secure, and not to rush back to work. He will always have a job."

Thank you, sir. That will mean a lot to him. He would like to come back but he is not ready yet. I am sure he will be someday soon."

"That brings me to the reason I asked you to come here. Your team stopped a major terrorist attack on our Capitol. What makes it so remarkable to me is that you had not real intelligence and got there in time without any preparation. No one in the intelligence community knew that there would be an attack, other than in the 50 capitols."

"Sir, it did not seem logical that a massive nationwide attack would spare DC. We figured that they would want not only maximum damage but as much news coverage as they could get. We considered several targets and guessed correctly."

"Tower," said the President, "I am giving you and your entire team the Public Safety Officer Medal of Valor. It is the highest award that I can give a law enforcement officer."

"Mr. President, we were just doing our job."

"Be that as it may, I still want you and your team to be recognized for your outstanding service and bravery."

Tower sat there a bit stunned. His team had been lucky and saved lives, that was his job. He belonged to the oldest federal law enforcement agency. It was founded in 1789. They took their job seriously. "Tower, this country faces a constant terrorist threat. I want you and your team to work directly for me. I want you to hunt down these terrorists before they kill more Americans. Our military does a good job, but they are not allowed to do law enforcement in the United States, with a few exceptions. You will have whatever you need and you will not be tied down with a lot of red tape. Take a few days, talk it over with your team. It will be hard work and a lot of hours and travel. Get back to me by next week." Tower stood, shook the President's hand and left the Oval Office. This was a lot to process. It would have to be a team decision.

Chapter Forty-Four

Commander Morgan walked into the team room. He saw Senior Chief Evans checking the batteries on his flashlight, satellite radio, and strobe beacons.

"Senior Chief, a word."

Evans got up and walked over to his boss. "What's up?" asked Evans.

"Get your team together. Mission brief in the conference room in one hour, don't be late."

"Where are we going?" asked the SEAL.

"Iran," came the answer. Morgan left the room. "Everyone listen up. Briefing in the conference room in one hour. Be there. Real world mission way outside the wire." Outside the wire was a term sometimes used to let troops know they were going into a hostile area.

Fifty minutes later, the team walked into the conference room. There were several unfamiliar faces. One person was in a business suit, but without a tie. The others were naval officers in their khaki service uniforms. Evans examined their ribbons. None were SEALs or even airborne qualified. None displayed any combat decorations. They all had the usual ribbons for doing a good job and going to different places in the world.

The team took their seats. Commander Morgan opened the briefing. "You have a mission go for immediate insertion into Iran. You will arrive by sub. Once there, you will enter a private home. The target is Mohammad Abu al-Fadi. He is an Iranian national. Your briefing packets have his picture and physical description. The packets also contain our best guess diagram of his home." Morgan looked at the CIA representative in the suit. "This guy is the mastermind behind the July 4th terrorist attack and the three shipborne terrorist attacks on Labor Day. He is responsible for hundreds of US deaths and probably several thousand injuries, not to mentions extensive property damage across the country. He is to be taken off the board." This could mean different things to different people but none of them good for him.

The first briefer stood up. "I am Captain Morrisson. I am the assistant staff weather officer from CENTCOM." The young Air Force officer went on. "In your packets, you will see the forecast for the next two weeks around Bandar Abbas, Iran. We expect the temperature to be in the mid-70s during the daytime and the mid 50s at night. There will be a new moon, so the only source of light will be the city itself. Winds will be out of the west at 5 to 10 knots. Are there any questions?" Everyone shook their heads no.

The second briefer went to the podium. "I am Navy Captain Fleming. I am the assistant J-2 for CENTCOM." Everyone knew that staff sections were divided by purpose. The J-2 would be intelligence. Within the J-2 section, there would be sections which dealt with security, both physical and cyber, targeting, training, operations etc. Having a Navy Captain, which was the same as a full colonel in the other Services, meaning some serious work was being put into the briefing. This also meant that this was a very high priority mission. He continued, "Ocean currents in the Bandar Abbas area are calm this time of year and we do not expect them to adversely affect your approach to the beach. The shore gradient is considered mild and should not interfere with your getting on to the beach itself. There are no Iranian military units located between where you are going to come ashore and the target location. There are civilian police patrols in the area. However, if they are alerted, you can expect a company sized infantry unit to arrive within five to ten minutes at the most. Please be quiet." His attempt at humor did not work. The target itself is a private home. It is over 5,000 square feet. It has three bedrooms, each with its own bathroom. There is also a living room, a large conference room and, of course, a kitchen. There is a three car garage attached to the house. Your target sometimes leaves his cars in the driveway. Your target lives alone and rarely entertains anyone at night. "Maybe that is why he is so angry," said one of the SEALs. There was a little laughter and a glare from Commander Morgan. The room instantly quieted. "If I may continue?" said Captain Fleming. "The house is protected by ten foot high walls. The walls are about a foot thick. The number of explosives needed to make a hole large enough for the team would awake the neighborhood and the local military. There is a tall metal gate which leads to the driveway. The gate is kept closed by hydraulic arms. However, the joint where the arms connect to the gate should be vulnerable. If the locks are cut, then the arms can be manually removed and the gate could be swung open. Of a larger concern are the armed guards which are constantly patrolling the property. They are armed with assault rifles and pistols. They all carry two way radios. An interesting note, the guards do not follow a fixed schedule. They roam about the property in no particular order. The only stationery guards are the two at the front gate. You should expect an additional four to six guards patrolling the grounds. They do not enter the house." Several of the SEALs made notes in their packets. It might not be possible to get past all the guards quietly. It would also be difficult silencing the guards without alerting anyone else. "Any questions?"

Operator Washington asked, "Sir, how current is this information, and has the target made any security changes since the ship attacks?"

"Excellent question. This information is less than a week old. We have detected no change in security since the failed attack. He must feel safe at home."

Next up was a Navy Commander. From the gold badge on his chest, he was obviously a submarine officer. "I am Commander Johnston. I am the skipper of the USS Flagstaff, an L.A. class sub. I will be your chauffer to and from the target area. Right now, my boat is being fitted with a SEAL Delivery Vehicle. You guys are going first class." Evans knew this 39 foot long mini sub could take his entire team almost up to the beach. While not very fast, about 6 mph, the sub would keep them warm and dry. It would also allow them to conserve their energy for the mission on land. Being electric, it made almost no noise and had no exhaust. This would make a stealth approach possible. This would greatly enhance the possibility of a successful mission. "My boat will be ready when you are." He looked at Commander Morgan. "Tomorrow or the next day?." Morgan looked at Evans. "Sir, we can go tomorrow. There will be several days of travel time for us to go over the mission. I understand this is a high priority mission and we do not want the target to escape." Everyone nodded. They would board the Flagstaff tomorrow, with their gear and head for Iran.

The team went back to their team area. They laid out weapons, ammo, knives, flashlights, radios, spare batteries, body armor, and helmets. There was their SCUBA gear. Each piece checked. Masks, breathing regulators, hoses and connections. Their life would depend on them. They also laid out clothes without any US markings. No rank, no service branch and not made in America. Tomorrow they would leave behind any personal pictures, papers, or identification. If the mission went bad, there would be no proof that they were American military invading Iran. They would not give the enemy a major propaganda win. They would go home for a few hours of sleep. Those with families would say they were away on a mission. They would not say where or what for. The families had gotten use to this. They knew this was part of being the wife of a Navy SEAL.

The next morning came early. The team had made it to the team area by 0600 hours. They immediately started to pack their gear into their back packs. Not everything would fit. Their SCUBA gear was checked again and packed into another bag. Commander Morgan walked into the team area. "Are your men ready?" "Yes sir," replied Evans. "Bob, this is a very important mission. You are striking back for all the death and injury from the July 4th attacks. This is also the guy who tried to blow up Savannah, Norfolk and New York. Get it done." "Aye aye" said Evans. "When will the vans be here to take us to the sub?" Morgan said, "The vans should be here between 0700 and 0715. You will move out at 0730." Last minute preparations were completed. "Guys, this will be a tough one. We do have surprise on our side. Let's do what we do."

At 0710, the team and their gear were outside the team building. The two black vans were pulling up in front of the building. The team split in two. Half the SEALs got into the first van. The remainder got into the second van. Within minutes, both vans were on their way to the dock area. It was a short drive. They were there within 15 minutes. They exited the vans, carrying their gear.

As they approached the Flagstaff, they saw the SDV mounted on the submarine. Compared to the submarine, the 39 foot long mini sub looked small. It was big enough to carry the team and their gear.

Evans was met at the gang plank by Commander Johnston. Evans stopped, came to attention and saluted.

"Sir, request permission to come aboard." Johnston returned the sharp salute and said, "Permission granted. The COB will show you your bunks and work area. The crew knows where we are going, but not why. I will tell them after you return to the boat. Evans and the team went aboard the sub. They followed the COB to a small area with 8 empty racks. There was a place to pile up their gear. Submarines are not known for being roomy. Evans and the team started to unpack their weapons and SCUBA gear. "Once we get underway, we will review the plan again."

The team could hear the crew moving around. A slight vibration could be felt. A few minutes later, the boat started to move. The movement was calm. The sub ran like a Swiss watch. After about an hour, they heard a klaxon sound. The sub was diving. The sub disappeared from the surface of the water. Even from the air, the sub was not visible. The team took out their operations plan. The reviewed the intelligence again. They knew it by heart, but errors could mean death. They were reviewing the floor plan of the house and photos of the walled structure around the house, when a young sailor came into their area. The SEALs immediately picked up the files and photos. This sailor did not have the need to know. "Senior Chief, if you wish, follow me to the gallery. We are having lunch." The team had lost all sense of time.

They were seated at a table in the galley. As he went through the serving line, Evans was impressed with the quantity of food he was served. He looked at the other sailor to see if he was getting special treatment. He was not. Evans sat with the rest of the team and ate in silence. They could not discuss the mission with anyone else on the boat. As they were finishing lunch, Commander Johnston walked up to them. "How was the food?" Evans replied that it was the best food he could remember having on any ship. Johnston told them that, "We go to sea and stay underwater for months. Without great food, we would have a munity on this boat." "Please give the cook our best, this is great," said Evans.

After lunch, they went back to their assigned area. Their gear was secure. However, they kept their briefing folders with them at all times. It would have been almost impossible to have a security breach while underwater. Professionals do not take chances.

Their routine for the next few days was the same. They stayed in their area except for eating. The food was constantly great. They reviewed their plan over and over. Each member of the team knew their part of the mission in their sleep. Each member also knew the duties and requirements of every other team member. If a member was lost or incapable of doing their part, another team member could instantly step in. This is the way of small unit special operations.

Commander Johnston advised them that they would be deploying at 0100 hours. That should take them no more than 15 minutes to load their gear and themselves aboard SDV. The mission called for the sub to stop about six miles from shore. The SEALs would take the SDV to a few hundred meters from shore. Then the SDV would be put on the bottom. The water was not dangerously deep. The SEALs, in their SCUBA gear, would exit the craft and swim underwater until they were on shore. Then it got interesting. Once on shore, the dangerous part would start. They would have to walk from the beach to the target location, get past the guards and enter the home. Once inside, the mission would be completed. Then all that was necessary was to get back to the beach, and swim out to the SDV. They had to get the SDV back to the sub and dock with it, so the sub could leave before day light. All the time neither the sub, the SDV or the SEALs could be detected. What could go wrong?

At 0045 hours, the team arrived at the docking area of the sub. They had all their gear. It took them the full 15 minutes to load the gear properly. The SDV had to be balanced. The gear had to be even spread out through the compartment. The team started to climb into the SDV. It would be a very tight fit. However, swimming six miles with the gear was not something they wanted to do, if they didn't have to. Commander Johnston approached and wish them good luck. "Please be back by 0521. That is sunrise and I do not want to fight it out with an Iranian destroyer. Once you get back, we still have to dock the SDV. That takes time. In an emergency, you could abandon the SDV and enter as swimmers. I would hate to give this technology to the Iranians." Evans smiled, "We will do our best," and gave a quick salute as he entered the SDV.

Once the team was inside, Evans signaled to release the docking clamps. The little vehicle moved slowly away from the sub.

"Everyone ready?" asked Evans, even though he knew the answer. Everyone gave a thumbs up signal. Evans started the electric engine and the SDV moved slowly on its northbound course. The SDV was not very fast. If attacked, the team would exit the craft and swim. This vehicle could not out run a fast canoe.

As they approached the shore, Evans watched the depth gauge. When the depth was about 50 feet, he slowed the craft down and let it sink to the bottom. Once on the bottom, he made sure everyone was ready and one last check of the equipment. Everyone gave a thumbs up and Evans broke the seal and let the ocean in. One by one, the team members exited the SDV into the dark waters.

Being a SEAL is not like normal SCUBA diving. Yes, they had masks, flippers, and air tanks, but they swam in total darkness and without making a sound. No flashlights were use to find the way or even to light up a compass. They also towed behind them a waterproof bag. These bags, while heavy, carried all their gear. The mission could not be completed without this gear. SEALs are trained to swim for endurance, not speed. The swim to the shore took ten minutes. When they came out of the water, they were not tired. They were pumped up, ready to complete the mission. They removed their masks, air tanks and flippers. These items were place on the beach.

"O'Connor, I want you to stay here and guard the gear. We will need it to get back to the SDV."

"Aw, come on, Senior Chief, I don't want to miss the party," O'Connor complained.

"Without this gear being kept safe, we will probably not make it back to the sub. If we are spotted, you will have to cover our rears while we run back to you. Get an H&K 7.62 from one of the bags," Evans said.

The nine-pound rifle fired the 7.62 mm cartridge. The weapon could fire one round at a time for increase accuracy or fully automatic. On full auto, the 20 round magazine would empty in about 2 to 3 seconds. Also, accuracy would be lost. Unlike some movies, these weapons could run out of ammunition. Carrying several hundred rounds of ammo would be quite heavy. The seven SEALs checked their weapons and gear. They were all heavily laden. Still, they moved out into the darkness.

Chapter Forty-Five

The seven SEALs walked quietly off the beach. They spread out a few yards between each man. If they were fired upon, they were not bunched up. A bullet meant for one man would not accidently hit another. No one talked. They didn't need to. They have gone over the plan over and over. If necessary, a hand signal would relay information. Sound was their enemy. They approached Ghadir Boulevard. This road ran parallel to the beach. In the day time, this road was crowded with all sorts of vehicles and pedestrians. Now, it was dead still. This is what the SEALs had hoped for. They all stopped and knelt before approaching the road. They check out the area and the possibility of traffic. A SEAL caught in the headlights of a passing car would be bad. Being seen by police or a military vehicle would be disaster. Their luck held and they quickly crossed the street.

They silently passed the park on its west side. Only a few lights were on in the park. Probably for security purposes. The SEALs were far enough away that the light did not cast a shadow on them They continued north. The had to be back to the sub before daylight. After a few minutes they could see the home, or at least the wall around it. To blast through the wall would awake the neighborhood. Even though there were few structures in the area, someone might hear it. They had considered using ropes and grappling hooks to scale the wall. A ten foot wall would be no challenge. The problems was going over the wall, providing security on both sides at the same time. Too many moving parts of an operation could lead to exposure and failure. The decided on the direct approach.

They had gotten to fifty yards of the front gate. Evans observed the two guards just inside the main gate. They were armed with assault rifles. Probably AK-47s. Not the latest model, but the AK-47 had been killing people for over seventy years. Not something to be taken lightly. Both Evans and Washington studied the guards through their night vision scopes. Neither appeared to be on alert. Both would be taken out at the same time. Using hand signals, Evans identified Washington's target to him. Evans gave a hand signal for a five second countdown. Both SEALs took aim at their target. They counted down to zero and fired. The silenced Heckler and Koch 416s fired at the same time. The bullets hit both guards at the same time. With lethal head shots, both dropped instantly. The only sound was the rifles hitting the driveway.

Evans gave the hand signal, and the team ran up to the front gate. As Special Warfare Operator 2nd class Willaims approached the gate, he was getting his small mini bolt cutter from his pack. He was heading directly for the gate when another guard appeared at the gate. Willaims had his hands full with the bolt cutter, as the guard raised his rifle. Two silenced rifles fired at the same time. The guard was hit in the chest and throat. He dropped his weapon, tried to grab his throat and collapsed. So much for CIA intelligence. Williams looks at Evans and Washington. They had just saved his life. A nod of appreciation was given. The team took care of their own.

Williams approached the double gate. Both sides of the gate were secured by a hydraulic arm. This arm would open the gate by pressing a remote button. The dead guards, one of whom probably had the button, were laying inside the fence. That would be no help. Willaims observed that the arms were locked in their pivot points by a heavy pad lock. While Willaims could not pick the locks, he could cut them. The mini bolt cutters cut through the hasps on both locks. Evans and Washington reached through the bars of the gate and pulled the hydraulic arm out of the pivot point. The gates swung open. The team was inside the compound.

Special Warfare Operator 1st Class Peterson was left at the front gate. He would sound the alert if the team had been discovered, He would have to hold off any police or military until the entire team could exit the house and regroup at the front gate. He also carried an H&K 7.62 rifle. While heavier to carry and providing more recoil, the 7.62 bullet had much more knockdown power than the 5.66 round shot from M-16 or M-4 rifles.

The remaining six SEALs headed for the house. Just as they were approaching the front door, a guard came around the corner of the house. He went for the pistol on his hip. He was too slow. Two bullets from Washington's silenced rifle struck him in the chest. One bullet cut a path through is left lung. The other bullet struck his heart.

He was dead before he hit the ground. The front door was locked. Normally, an explosive charge would open the door. Barring that method, a shotgun blast to the lock or door hinges would solve the problem. Those methods could not be used here. Silence was paramount. Chief Sam Roberts, the team's second in command was an expert with lock picks. He always complained that never got to use his picks as doors were always being blown open. Now he had his chance. On one knee, Roberts worked the two small metal picks in the key hole. Roberts thought what a cheap door lock. Then again, men roaming the grounds with assault rifles should keep most burglars away. There was a click and the door was open.

The team, with their night vision goggles on, entered the house. Their weapons were up and ready. No one on the team knew exactly what to expect. They broke down into three teams of two men each. They would search the house. There was no way of knowing if anyone else was spending the night there. Intelligence reports said he did not have a girlfriend. Reports could be wrong. One team cleared the kitchen and living room area. Other than some high end furniture, there was noting of interest there. The other two teams checked the three bedrooms and their adjoining bathrooms. The first bedroom was set up as a private office. There were numerous books on wooden shelves, a computer was on the desk. The computer was hooked to an external hard drive. Roberts disconnected it and put it in his backpack. There might be some intelligence of value on it. Evans' team cleared another bedroom at the same time. It was set up as a guest room. There was no sign that it had been recently used.

Evans and Roberts both got to the last bedroom at the same time. They looked at each other. They both hoped that the target was in there. They were running out of time and places to look. If he was not home, this mission would be a total failure at best and an international incident at worst. Evans and Washington kneeled in front of the door. Roberts stood at the side of the door. Roberts looked at Evans. Evans gave him a nod. Roberts slowly started to turn the door knob.

The sound of gunfire from inside the room shattered the silence. Two holes appeared in the door at chest height. If the two SEALs had been standing in front of the door, instead of kneeling, the bullets would have certainly struck them. Roberts quickly turned the knob and threw the door open. Mohammad Abu al-Fadi stood next to the bed. He was in his pajamas. He had a dark colored pistol in his hand. The sight of the four SEALs, in full combat gear, at his doorway, none apparently hit by his bullets, startled him for a second. It was a second that he did not have. Evans and Washington fired at the same time, two rounds each. Both double taps hit their target in the middle of his chest. There was no chance of survival. His limp body felon the floor. Evans ran up to him. No pulse, no breathing, mission accomplished. Evans took a small digital camera from one of his pockets and took a few pictures. The brass would want proof of the accomplishment.

Evans gave a hand gesture, and the two teams ran towards the front door. It was time to leave. As they approached the front door, they were joined by the third team. They exited the front of the house and almost ran into another guard. Without slowing or breaking their stride, the guard was shot by several of the SEALs. They ran out, past the gate and headed for the beach. It was getting late and sunrise would be in about an hour. Somehow, they were behind schedule. They retraced their steps back to the beach. There was now traffic on Ghadir Boulevard. They could not cross as a group. Seven men in black tactical gear and swim suits might attract attention. When there were breaks in the traffic, they would cross in ones and twos. This crossing also slowed them down.

They reached the beach. O'Connor was there with their gear. They quickly put their SCUBA gear on and secured their weapons and equipment in the waterproof bags. Evans looked at his watch and cursed. They were behind schedule. Commander Johnston would not be happy.

The SEALs entered the water and swam underwater back to the SDV. Their breathing equipment was self-contained and would not leave a trail of bubbles behind them to show the enemy where to look and shoot. Now they were swimming for speed. They knew where they were going and how dangerous it would be if they were late. Would the sub wait? Could an Iranian warship be in the area? Evans did not know. They found the SDV and, one at a time, entered the vehicle and stowed their gear. As the last man got on board, the hatch was sealed. Evans fired up the engine and the vessel started to move. Evan plotted a direct course back to the sub and set the engine for full speed.

"Conn, Sonar, picking up a faint sound. It could be the SDV. Whatever it is, it is heading this way."

Johnston looked at his watch. They were running late, and daylight was almost here. While they would not be visible from the shore, Johnston knew that Iranian patrol boats increased their patrolling at dawn. His boat was ready to clamp on to the SDV and get the SEALs aboard. He would then move out into the Straits of Hormuz and head home. He could easily navigate around the Iranian islands, which lay between the coast and the Straits.

"Conn, Sonar, Picking up another contact. Surface ship, course 120, speed 10 knots. She is heading in our general direction. It is not a cargo ship. She is along ways off, just at our limit of discovery."

"Keep me advised every minute. Where the hell is Evans?" he asked to no one in particular. He did not want to get in a battle with the Iranian Navy.

Evans and the team were about a minute away from the sub. They still could not see the sub in the dark waters. Finally, he saw the sub. He looked at his watch. Johnston is going to be very upset. Evans maneuvered the SDV over the hatch and let the mini-sub touch the top of the Flagstaff. He immediately activated the docking clamps. As they opened the hatch, the sub's hatch also opened. They quickly exited the SDV and entered the sub.

"Request permission to come aboard," Evans said in a light-hearted tone.

"Granted, did you guys stop for a beer or what? Johnston asked in a sarcastic tone.

"No, Sir, we would not want to miss your great chow. Mission accomplished."

"Get to your space and secure your gear. We may have company in a few minutes" said Johnston.

Evans felt a pain in his gut. Did their lateness put the sub and its crew at risk? Worse, he knew there was nothing he could do to help. He and the teams went to the area set aside for them. They got strange looks from the crew as they walked through the boat. Was it envy or anger? He would not ask. They got to their area and secured their gear. They would clean their weapons once they were safely underway. Evans knew that like SEALs, the subs best defense was silence. There would be no unnecessary movement on the boat. To reenforce that thought, the boat's speakers announced, "Rigg for silent running. Ultras quiet"

With that, a strange silence filled the boat. No one talked. No one moved unless absolutely necessary. All lose items were secured. A cooking pot hitting the deck during a maneuver could kill them all. Evans could feel the boat start to turn. He could also feel the boat move. It was not going anywhere full speed. That would be noisy.

"Conn, Sonar. Surface now closing at 15 knots, range 25,000 yards. Probably a Kaman fast attack boat. Its top speed is 36 knots and she is equipped with harpoon style missiles."

Johnston knew he could sink the Kaman, but really did not want to. He also knew if he tried to outrun her, the sub's cavitation sounds would give them away. Cavitation is caused by the propeller or screw as it is called on ships, disturbing the water. Speed and depth had an effect on how loud it would sound to the surface ship. They would know it was a sub and not one of theirs.

"Helm, all ahead one third. Make your depth 50 feet above the ocean bottom," was Johnston's order.

The helmsman, a young sailor, had never done that before. Hitting the bottom would damage the sub and the sound would let everyone know there the sub was.

The COB walked up to the helmsman, put a hand on his shoulder, and calmly said, "You can do this."

The boat was now moving and hugging the bottom. If it was possible, everyone was holding their breath. The sub could not go to battle stations for fear of letting the Kaman know they were there.

"Conn, Sonar, range is now 20,000 yards and still closing."

The boat continued to move through the dark waters. The sun was coming up, but that should not help the Kaman. She would use sonar to locate the sub.

As the Flagstaff continued southward, the ocean floor dropped away. The young helmsman adjusted the boat, and she went deeper into the darkness.

"Conn, Sonar, range is 15,000 yards and closing. Sir, they are actively pinging. The surface ship was using its sonar to find the sub.

"I wonder if they know we are here, or is this some proactive patrol technique? Increase speed to 2/3," said Johnston. He hoped the sound would not give them away.

"Conn, Sonar, range is now at 20,000 yards. We are pulling away. No active sonar."

"They were fishing," said Johnston.

Evans and his team relaxed. They feared their delay might have spelled disaster for the crew and the sub. Dying was one thing. Getting others killed was another thing.

There was almost an audible sigh as the crew relaxed. It would take them several days to return to base. Once the Flagstaff was further away from the Iranian coast, they would advise CENTCOM of mission success. While the Iranians would not be able to understand, an electronic broadcast might alert their navy. It was not worth the risk. The crew would get some well deserved shore leave. The SEALs would go back to the base and be get ready for the next mission. The President would go on national television and tell the American people that the man who tried to cripple American and who was responsible for the death and injury of so many was dead. The heroes who planned, coordinated, and had risked their lives to accomplish this feat would only be known to a few. That was enough.

About The Author

Marc Neerman is a retired Army Colonel. His career spans almost 40 years. He has served from Southeast Asia to the Middle East. He has served as an intelligence officer from the battalion to the national level. Many of his assignments have been with airborne and special operations units. He has been an instructor at the Army's Intelligence School, the Special Warfare Center, and the National Defense University.